MW01223618

GRACE

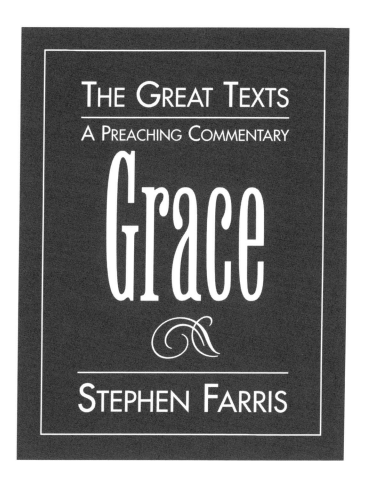

THE GREAT TEXTS

A PREACHING COMMENTARY

Grace

STEPHEN FARRIS

Abingdon Press
Nashville

THE GREAT TEXTS SERIES

GRACE
A PREACHING COMMENTARY

Copyright © 2003 by Abingdon Press

All rights reserved.
No part of this work may be reproduced or transmitted in any form or by any means, electronic or mechanical, including photocopying and recording, or by any information storage or retrieval system, except as may be expressly permitted by the 1976 Copyright Act or in writing from the publisher. Requests for permission should be addressed to Abingdon Press, P.O. Box 801, 201 Eighth Avenue South, Nashville, TN 37202-0801, or permissions@abingdonpress.com.

This book is printed on acid-free paper.

Library of Congress Cataloging-in-Publication Data

Farris, Stephen.
  Grace : a preaching commentary / Stephen Farris.
     p. cm.
Includes bibliographical references.
  ISBN 0-687-09046-6 (alk. paper)
  1. Grace (Theology)—Biblical teaching.   2. Bible—Homiletical use.
I. Title.

  BS680.G7F37 2003
  234—dc22

2003013901

All scripture quotations unless noted otherwise are taken from the New Revised Standard Version of the Bible, copyright 1989 by the Division of Christian Education of the National Council of the Churches of Christ in the United States of America. Used by permission. All rights reserved.

Scripture quotations noted KJV are taken from the King James or Authorized Version of the Bible.

Scripture quotations noted NIV are taken from the HOLY BIBLE: NEW INTERNATIONAL VERSION®. Copyright © 1973, 1978, 1984 by the International Bible Society. Used by permission of Zondervan Publishing House. All rights reserved.

Scripture quotations noted RSV are taken from the Revised Standard Version of the Bible, copyright 1946, 1952, 1971 by the Division of Christian Education of the National Council of the Churches of Christ in the United States of America. Used by permission. All rights reserved.

Lines from the poem "Putting the Amazing Back in Grace" on page 93 are from *Putting the Amazing Back in Grace* by Ann Weems. © 1999 by Ann Barr Weems. Used by permission of Westminster John Knox Press.

03 04 05 06 07 08 09 10 11 12—10 9 8 7 6 5 4 3 2 1

MANUFACTURED IN THE UNITED STATES OF AMERICA

Contents

Acknowledgments

I could not write of grace if I had not first received it on every hand. Grace cannot be earned, but it can and must be acknowledged. It is my pleasant duty, therefore, to thank at least some of those who have been agents of grace for me in this undertaking. I am grateful to the staff of Abingdon Press for their patience and encouragement. In particular, I must mention John Holbert, the editor of this series, a friend as well as an editor, and Bob Ratcliff, editor at Abingdon Press. I also thank my friend and colleague in Toronto, Paul Scott Wilson, for reading and commenting on the manuscript and also my excellent teaching assistant, Emily Rodgers. Needless to say, any remaining errors and infelicities are my own fault, my own grievous fault.

This material has been "tried out" repeatedly in many churches and classrooms. In particular, I must thank in this connection the president and faculty of the Atlantic School of Theology, Halifax, Nova Scotia, for inviting me to deliver the C. M. Newton Lectures, the seeds around which this book grew. I never saw the sun shine in Halifax, but I was always warmed by their hospitality. I cannot name here all the churches and ministers who gave me the opportunity to preach grace from their pulpits. I would be remiss, however, if I did not mention Yorkminster Park Baptist Church in Toronto and its senior minister, Peter Holmes. Almost they persuaded me to become a Baptist! I think "Linda" would be embarrassed if I named her or her church, but I am truly grateful. My own minister, Douglas Rollwage, would not be embarrassed in the least to be named here. I quote a line from one of his sermons in the book. I am chiefly grateful, however, that when I attend my home church, I hear grace preached.

Above all I thank my wife, Patty. She is constant grace to me. I have learned much about grace from my two sons, Allan and Daniel. I am absurdly proud of them.

Two people first taught me grace: Muriel Caroline Neale Farris, loving and patient mother, and Allan Leonard Farris, caring father and preacher of the gospel of grace, now at rest. They brought me up "in the nurture and admonition of the Lord," and to them I dedicate this book.

Introduction

"Let the little children come to me; do not stop them; for it is to such as these that the kingdom of God belongs. Truly I tell you, whoever, does not receive the kingdom of God as a little child will never enter it." Mark 10:14b-15

Some of my seminary classmates may recall the story differently, but this is the way I remember it happening. We were sitting in New Testament class under Professor Balmer Kelly when this text came up for discussion. Professor Kelly turned to us and said, "Why like a little child?"[1]

One student raised a hand and asserted with considerable confidence, "Because little children are so naturally good and innocent."

Professor Kelly simply replied, "You don't have any children yet, do you?" It was true; that particular student had no children, and any parent could have refuted the notion from repeated experience.

Somebody else ventured another answer, "Because children are all humble."

Professor Kelly stroked his beard and asked, "Have you ever stood outside a schoolyard during recess and listened to the children?" We all thought back to our grade-school days: "I'm the king of the castle and you're the dirty rascal!" That answer was, by common accord, dismissed without a further thought. Several more possibilities were raised, each more unlikely than the last. Finally Professor Kelly looked at us with suitable professorial disgust. He reached into his pocket, pulled out his wallet, and extracted a twenty-dollar bill. He walked over to a student named Don, the toughest, most hard-nosed man in the class, and gave the bill to him. Don turned approximately the shade of a Canadian Mountie's dress uniform.

"You don't like me giving you money, do you?" said Professor Kelly. "You're going to try to give it back to me after the class, but I'm not going to take it." That Don didn't like it was manifest; he was holding the bill by its absolute tip as if it were covered with a particularly nasty acid that was burning the tips of his fingers.

"Now if I asked you to come over to my house to do some yard work or to help me move some books and I paid you for your work, you wouldn't mind at all." There were nods of agreement all around.

"But what if I gave the money to a child?"

No further words were necessary for the picture of a child reaching out a hand to receive what had not been earned, a child who thought it the most natural thing in the world to receive a gift, that picture was there before us.

Whoever does not receive the kingdom of God as a little child . . .

"Receive" may be the key word in the text. It's not easy for us adults to receive. Our society teaches us that we must earn our way, that we must get ahead by our own efforts. The church often simply reinforces that message. In church we are most often taught to *give*. We are oriented in the church to giving—our time, our money, our commitment. Much of preaching is aimed at motivating people to give, once again not just money. If nothing else, we urge people at least to give a damn, though hardly ever in exactly those words. And, of course, we preachers are givers. We have given our lives to Christ. We give our days and most of our evenings to the service of the church. We value ourselves, to a large extent, by what we have given. It may be more blessed to give than to receive, but it is also a whole lot easier. Grace sounds simple, but it is difficult, childishly difficult. Before we can give, we must receive, and grace is about receiving. Perhaps one reason it is difficult to preach grace may simply be that very few preachers are children.

We religious people may even fear grace in our heart of hearts. We would rather depend on our own performance. After all, this gives us credit that is denied to others. Perhaps this practical denial of grace comes from a fear of placing ourselves at the mercy of another, even of Another our creeds and hymns claim to be totally good. "Perfect love casts out fear" is written in 1 John 4:18. But the presence of fear prevents the possibility of a love that will truly place oneself and one's fate in the hands of another. It is hard for fearful creatures to receive grace.

Perhaps it is hard to receive grace because we religious folk want there to be a moral standard to which we want everyone—even God—to adhere as if there could be some standard outside God to which God must bow. Grace, whatever it is, isn't very fair by the standards we would design. "I will have mercy on those whom I will have mercy," says the Lord. Where is the justice in that? We want a world that adheres to our notions of justice and fairness, a justice in which we receive the rewards due our goodness. And others? Well, they get what is coming to them too. Not only is grace not quite fair, but also it isn't even very moral. We preachers are mostly moral people, and grace seems suspiciously amoral. We empathize with the older brother in the great parable: "All these years, I have slaved for you . . . but this son of yours" (my translation). Anders Nygren retells that old story, so that it speaks of:

a father whose son had wasted his substance with riotous living in a far country and then returned to his father destitute but with good intentions; but the father, who knew from experience what such good intentions are usually worth, met the son's entreaties with the stern reply, "My house is closed to you until by your own honest work you have earned a place for yourself and so made amends for the wrong you have done"; and the son went out into the world and turned over a new leaf and when he afterwards returned to his father he thanked him for the unyielding severity that had led to his recovery, unlike the foolish softness and weak indulgence of some other fathers, which would have let him continue in his prodigal ways.[2]

Surely that version of the parable is far more moral (and believable in an age of "tough love") than the way Jesus tells it!

At the very least, grace is frighteningly arbitrary, and we moral folk prefer the safely predictable. Well did C. S. Lewis represent the Christ figure, the fount of grace, by a lion in his Narnia tales. When human children are taken to Narnia, they hear of Aslan, the great lion. Inevitably they ask, "Is he safe?" "No, but he is good," is the reply. Grace is dangerous and we prefer safety. True goodness is often a little bit dangerous, and we religious folk often like to play it safe. Whatever the reason we flee, both spiritually and homiletically, from grace and seek another reality in which to place our trust.

If it is difficult simply to receive grace, it seems equally difficult to preach it. There are many tempting alternatives to preaching grace. Why Christian preachers should be so tempted to preach something other than grace is a mystery but so it is. It is difficult to preach grace because both those who preach and those who hear are human beings and, even worse, are religious.

Every once in a while I do a little exercise with a student sermon. I take a red pen and underline every instance of "We ought," "We must," "God calls us to . . . ," "Our responsibility is . . . " on the last page of the sermon. There's a lot of red ink. It is as if we preachers believe we meet God only as demand. It is as if we Christians are the subjects of all the key verbs and carry out all the important actions. The subject of grace, by contrast, is God.

But at least seminary students have an excuse; they're still learning. I fear, however, that what is true of student sermons is true of ministerial sermons as well. Indeed that is why students preach the way they do. They preach what they have heard all their lives.[3] David Buttrick's complaint may be more true than we like to admit:

> Sermons fail to mediate the presence and the grace of God. Many sermons are moral exhortations, which can be heard delivered with greater skill at the Rotary or Kiwanis Club. Many sermons are political

and economic judgments on society, which have been presented with greater wisdom and passion at political conventions. Many sermons offer personal therapies which can be better provided by well-trained psychiatrists.[4]

All this has produced some highly negative evaluations of preaching. I was a high school classmate of my future brother-in-law, David.[5] About the time I got my present job, David was at the family summer cottage with yet another former high school classmate.

"What is Steve doing these days?" asked the classmate.

"He's just got a job as a professor of homiletics," answered David.

"What's homiletics?"

"I don't know, exactly," confessed David.

He went to the bookcase and pulled down the well-worn *Concise Oxford Dictionary* we use to settle spelling arguments in Scrabble games. *Homiletics* didn't appear in that edition of the dictionary, but *homily* did. The second entry under the word *homily* read "a tedious moralizing discourse"!

Nor are the usual Protestant words any better received than *homily*. When a teenager says "Don't preach to me! I don't want a sermon," we know exactly what the teen means. What did we preachers do to make people think that way about preaching? To preach grace means to announce God's free, undeserved love and favor. We know the depth of that love because of the cross and the power of that love because of the resurrection. Perhaps if we actually preached grace, our society—perhaps even our teenagers—would not think so ill of preaching.

This, then, is a book about preaching grace, that is, about *proclaiming the free and unmerited love and mercy of God*. Though from time to time a story about grace will appear, as in this introduction, this book is not intended to be a collection of quotations and anecdotes.[6] Nor is it a theological treatise on grace and its relation to the preaching task.[7] In the title of this book and series are the words *texts* and *commentary*. A commentary is a book that contains the results of the study of *texts*. I am at heart a preacher, and I intend to do what preachers do week by week, namely, wrestle with texts. Wrestle along with me. Perhaps we will limp away with a blessing, a blessing named grace.

Before beginning our wrestling, several preliminary matters must be noted. In the first place, our primary encounter is not with the secondary literature (though it has been consulted); it is with the text itself. Moreover, we will be dealing primarily with the text as it stands and in its canonical context. Some classic historical-critical questions will be considered, a few in some detail, but only insofar as they bear directly on our theological understanding of the text. We will take note of literary themes and motifs, especially in the narrative texts, but not because the literary structure of the text is inherently more interesting than its prehistory. It is because the literary themes and motifs of a book as intensely theological as the Bible are themselves likely to be theologically significant. The key word here is *theological.* A reading of Scripture for the purpose of preaching grace will be at heart theological.

There is another key word in the title of this book, *preaching.* A reading of a text for preaching ought to be not only theological, but also personal. A coolly academic, unbiased, distanced study of a text—the aim of older scholarship—is now widely considered to be a false goal. The person and situation of the reader shape all readings. No one reads a text from a position of neutrality. Even aside from obvious biases, we bring to each text a *preunderstanding* of its nature and significance. I bring this preunderstanding: The text is above all a means by which God addresses me in my lostness with a word that is at once acceptance, rebuke, demand, and ultimate hope.

If we leave matters there, however, we have been far too individualistic. The Bible is the church's book. It came into being in communities of faith, has been treasured there and attended to there. It addresses not only me as an individual, but also the church as a whole. One of the chief ways, perhaps the foremost way, that the Bible addresses the church is through preaching. A *preaching* commentary will seek in the texts it studies a word from God for the church. Our reading of texts must be theological, personal, and ecclesial.

Such a reading ought, however, to be churchly but not "churchy." The mission of God, of which preaching is a part, works through the church to the world. An "in-house" reading of the Bible is, by nature, inadequate. Preaching that speaks only of the affairs and preoccupations of the church itself and of its individual members is but a feeble instrument for the mission of God. To put it simply, grace comes not only to members of the church, but also to all creation.

Perhaps a series of optical images will be helpful here. The task of a commentary is to examine the text. Imagine the commentator inviting the reader to look closely at the text as if through the lens of a magnifying glass. We employ various literary and historical techniques as our lenses.[8] One might also compare our fundamental understanding of what the Bible teaches and is to a lens. Using these sorts of lenses, the biblical scholar and the preacher look *at* the text.

If, however, that second sort of lens, our fundamental understanding of the Bible, includes the conviction that God addresses us through the texts of Scripture, the whole process reverses itself. We might begin to sense as we read the text that God is examining us and inviting us to share in that examination. Now the Bible might become another sort of optical device, namely, a mirror. In the text, we see ourselves more clearly, perhaps for the first time. Moreover, to return for a moment to the image of a lens, we can now understand that the text itself might become a lens. Now, however, we look *through* the text rather than at it. Through the lens of the text we perceive a picture of the world clearer than was available to us previously. But if our lens is very clear and if we look very faithfully through it, we might catch sight of something far more significant than the world alone. Through the lens of the text, we might even see God in Christ acting through the power of the Holy Spirit in that world.[9]

In commentary on preaching *grace*, we will be examining our texts for grace and using our texts to see the work of grace in the world and in ourselves. Grace is *the free and unmerited love and mercy of God*. We cannot speak of this grace, however, without also saying, and saying clearly, that this free gift demands a costly discipleship. Dietrich Bonhoeffer has taught us the dangers of "cheap grace": "Cheap grace is the grace we bestow on ourselves. Cheap grace is the preaching of forgiveness without requiring repentance, baptism without church discipline, Communion without confession, absolution without personal confession."[10]

Grace is free but is never cheap. We meet God not only as total acceptance, but also as total demand. Bonhoeffer was right: Preaching that does not honestly lay before the people the demand of God is nothing but cheap grace. But demand that does not rest on grace is legalism. We will pay attention to the demand of the text but will always note that demand rests upon grace. The one who says, "You shall have no other gods before me" (Exod. 20:3) is the one who first says, "I am the LORD your God, who brought you up out of the land of Egypt" (Exod. 20:2). Jesus said, "Come to me, all you that are weary and are carrying heavy burdens, and I will give you rest" (Matt. 11:28). But he also said, "Take my yoke upon you, and learn from me" (Matt. 11.29). Grace without demand is cheap; demand without grace is a dreadful burden. Grace and demand cannot rightly be separated in the preaching of the gospel of Jesus Christ. Indeed, as we shall see, the demand of a gracious God is itself grace: "For my yoke is easy, and my burden is light" (Matt. 11:30).

There is another problem facing anyone who would write or preach on grace. It is dangerously easy to get slightly but dangerously wrong the business of grace as undeserved or unmerited love. This problem was drawn forcibly to my attention when my local newspaper carried an odd story several years ago. Here it is:

> An estimated 100,000 Japanese are worrying about the weight of their souls, rather than their bodies. Their guru, former baby care specialist Yugi Taniguchi, has told them that if their inner spirits are heavier than 10 kilograms, they will die before the end of May. However, those with

lighter souls will be rescued by a giant spaceship that can carry 100 million passengers, according to a channeled space alien called Maria. People will reduce the weight of their souls, Mr. Taniguchi claims, if they practice chanting: "What's your name? I feel wretched about myself, oh yay, yay."[11]

There are Christian equivalents to this that are only marginally less loopy. Preaching grace does not mean making people feel wretched about themselves. Indeed, in the end, the opposite is true. We know we are of immense worth precisely because of grace. If we have been grasped by grace, we know that God loves us with a passion and a depth beyond our power fully to conceive. People who are loved like this know they are not worthless.

THE TEXTS

In the end, the only justification for selecting the particular texts to be studied in this book lies within the studies themselves. The reader may appreciate a few preliminary words, however. With respect to the New Testament, *grace* is in large measure Paul's word (see the statistics in the next chapter). For that reason, the first section of the book deals with three texts from Paul or Paul's followers. Two of those include classic Sunday school memory work and statements about grace—2 Corinthians 8:9 and Ephesians 2:10. The third, a study of Philemon, takes as its starting point Paul's most typical use of the word *grace* in his greetings and farewells. But what Paul means by grace is omnipresent in Scripture. The reality of grace can be found everywhere in it. We will therefore look to preach grace from texts in which the word itself does not appear. The word *grace* appears only infrequently in the Gospels, but grace is manifestly at work within them. The second section of the book is a study of four Gospel pericopes. The prologue to the Gospel of John reminds us that in Jesus we behold a glory "as of a father's only son, full of grace and truth" (John 1:14). We will first look for that grace and truth in a representative pericope from that Gospel, the healing of a paralytic in John 5. Turning to the Gospel of Luke, we will examine a classic story of grace, Jesus' encounter with Zacchaeus in Luke 19:1-10. There follows an attempt to see grace in the parable of the pounds, in Luke 19:11-27, which is almost invariably preached as obligation. Perhaps it is possible to preach grace from "obligation" texts as well. I did not expect to include in the book another Gospel text, Jesus' encounter with the Syro-Phoenician woman in Mark 7. I was surprised.

Some Christians imagine that grace belongs to the New Testament while the Old Testament knows only law. This is, of course, pernicious nonsense. The Old Testament is suffused with grace, even though the Hebrew word for grace does not appear. We see it very early in the story of God's treatment of the first murderer, Abel, and also in the healing of a foreign general, Naaman. Surprisingly, it is also there in the praise of the law of God in Psalm 119 and the prophet's call for justice in Isaiah 58. Grace arches over the older testament like a rainbow.

Grace in Paul and His Followers

CHAPTER 1

2 Corinthians 8:7-15:
You Know the Grace of Our Lord Jesus

Many of us will remember from our childhoods those Bibles in which the words of Jesus were printed in red ink. Those words, it was implicitly understood, were uniquely important and valuable beyond the words that came from the early church only. With a more sophisticated understanding of how the Gospels came to be, and perhaps because of printing costs, the practice has become less common. It has had a fascinating revival in recent years, however. The Jesus Seminar printed in red ink those words of Jesus and reports about him that passed their tests for historical authenticity. It is not my intention to discuss the work of the Jesus Seminar here, but rather to recall to our minds this image of printing with red letters to lift the essential from the background and to highlight the uniquely important. In that sense, the word *grace* might be printed in red in the apostle Paul. For him it is a red-letter doctrine. When preaching from Paul, it is always wise to look for grace.

Without some version of "red ink" for grace, we might miss the importance of the word in Paul's writings. We might suppose, for example, that Paul's letters focus on the doctrine of justification by faith, or we might consider Paul primarily a pastoral theologian dealing with the problems of early Christian congregations. Neither approach would be an error. Justification by faith is indeed central, at least in Romans and Galatians, and Paul is a pastoral theologian through and through. But it is in the *grace* of God made known in the cross and resurrection that we are to place our faith. It is *grace* that shapes the church and gives it an identity. The church's calling is to live up to that grace-filled identity.

Even where the word *grace* is not present in Paul, the reality of grace is never far off.

The word *grace* itself is obviously important to Paul, however. *Charis*, the Greek word for *grace*, never appears in Matthew and Mark, appears eight times in Luke and four times in John (all in the *logos* hymn) but twenty-six times in the letter to the Romans alone. Moreover, the word appears no less than ten times in our text and its surrounding material—the discussion of the collection for the saints in Jerusalem in 2 Corinthians 8 and 9—though that is not immediately obvious from some of our English translations. In other words, there are almost as many appearances of the word *grace* in these two short chapters as in the four Gospels put together. Furthermore, as we shall see in the next chapter of this book, all Paul's letters are framed by the word *grace*. If we sing "Amazing Grace" as a favorite hymn, it is partly because grace was a favorite word of the apostle Paul.

THE LIMITS AND CONTEXT OF THE PASSAGE

Our text is part not just of a single letter, but of a correspondence. We know of at least four letters from Paul to the Corinthians. The first was a letter, now lost, of pastoral advice from Paul to the Corinthians. Paul himself mentions this letter in 1 Corinthians 5:9. Apparently this letter raised as many questions among the Corinthians as it answered. The Corinthians then wrote back to Paul asking for clarification (1 Cor. 7:1). Our 1 Corinthians is Paul's reply. At some point after 1 Corinthians arrived at its destination, the always complex relationship between Paul and the Corinthians deteriorated. Paul then wrote a "letter of tears," mentioned in 2 Corinthians 7:8-9. Many scholars suppose that the present 2 Corinthians 10–13 is the core of this stern letter.[1] There then followed our 2 Corinthians in whole or in part. In short, our 2 Corinthians is actually *fourth* Corinthians at least.

Moreover, 2 Corinthians has been for several centuries the happy hunting ground of source theorists. Various scholars have dissected that epistle into several different individual letters. Among the many theories is one that considers 2 Corinthians 8 part of a separate business letter. Some scholars argue that it preceded the present 2 Corinthians 9, which is manifestly about the same subject, the collection for the poor saints in Jerusalem; others suggest that it originally followed that chapter. Still other scholars argue that 2 Corinthians is a unity as it stands.[2] Fortunately the preacher does not need to solve these problems in a sermon. We can say with confidence from the pulpit that our text is part of an appeal on behalf of the impoverished saints of the church of Jerusalem that extends through all our present 2 Corinthians 8 and 9. These two chapters are recognizable enough as a unit that they are the sole subject matter of their own commentary, a highly unusual phenomenon in biblical studies.[3] These two chapters may have formed part or parts of a separate business letter that was combined into our present 2 Corinthians, but that is not a significant point for preaching purposes. What may be more significant is this: One cannot speak or write about the weightier matters of the Christian faith for any sustained period without eventually reaching the topic of money. When Paul talks about money in our text, he talks about it in the context of grace.

Cutting a text into units is rarely as easy with Paul as it often is with other parts of Scripture. It would be ideal to read those two chapters as a whole, but that would doubtless try the patience of most contemporary churchgoers. Choosing some smaller unit of thought is therefore necessary. Within these two chapters, several divisions are possible. The Revised Common Lectionary, however, has selected as the reading for the sixth Sunday after Pentecost in Year B 2 Corinthians 8:7-15. This particular division is justifiable in that Paul turns from a discussion of Titus's work directly to the Corinthians in verse 7. At verse 15, Paul concludes a brief general defense of the fundamental fairness of his appeal. The material between those two markers forms Paul's attempt "to stir up the Corinthians to this good work of charity."[4]

At this point in the epistle, Paul is raising money for "foreign" purposes. To be more specific, the money is intended for "the poor among the saints at Jerusalem" (Rom 15:26) who, for reasons not specifically known to us, must have been undergoing difficulties. Paul refers to this offering at a number of points in his letters (see Rom. 15:25-27, 31; Gal. 2:10; 1 Cor. 16:1-4; and also Acts 24:17). Paul's motivation in all this is unknown. Perhaps he hoped that a generous gift would show the sincerity and genuine Christian commitment of his Gentile converts and thus serve as a validation of the gospel Paul has preached. Perhaps the offering would show in a tangible way that the hostility between Jew and Gentile was now being broken down. It has even been argued that this offering from the Gentiles symbolized in Paul's mind the tribute of the Gentiles to Zion that was expected in the last days. Or perhaps Paul was simply and genuinely moved by the suffering of the Christians of Jerusalem to whom all Gentile Christians owed their very lives in the faith. Whatever the motivation, the appeal is a matter of immense concern for the apostle.

Jews in the Diaspora sent money to support the Temple, and local almsgiving was a characteristic of Jewish communities. Consequently, an appeal to support coreligionists in Jerusalem might not have seemed strange to Jewish Christians. To us also this kind of appeal is such an ordinary and constant phenomenon that our responses may be nothing more than a shrug of the shoulders. The shrug may accompany a token gift, perhaps aimed primarily at getting the one who asks off our backs and off our consciences. Consequently, we might miss how strange and revolutionary this appeal must have been to the Gentile Christians in Corinth. This may have been the first such appeal in the history of the Gentile Christian church.

It is interesting to note that Paul begins his appeal with a technique that is still practiced, a challenge. He writes: "We want you to know, brothers and sisters, about the grace of God that has been granted to the churches of Macedonia" (2 Cor. 8:1). One can hear this kind of challenge on most charity telethons to this very day. As part of this challenge, Paul writes pointedly of the generosity of the Macedonian Christians. The Corinthians are, it appears, aware of the poverty of that church. Paul, however, emphasizes not their poverty, but their great generosity. Paul later writes that he boasts of the Corinthians to the Macedonians (2 Cor. 9:1), but the implication at this point is quite clear: The Corinthians must not fall behind their northern neighbors in their beneficence. There is certainly nothing shameful in writing or preaching about money; fundraising is necessary in churches ancient and modern alike. Moreover, we might honestly admit that Christians have always been stirred by the example of other Christians in giving, as well as in other aspects of the Christian life. One might even consider this an outworking of the doctrine of the communion of saints.

We ought also to note that in the verses leading to our passage, Paul repeatedly uses the word *grace*. We have seen how he begins his appeal: "We want you to know, brothers and sisters, about the grace of God that has been granted to the churches of Macedonia" (2 Cor. 8:1). Unfortunately, for those using only English translations, the other instances of the word *grace* may be obscured by a series of paraphrases. The Macedonians begged Paul earnestly for the "grace" (NRSV and NIV, "privilege"; RSV, "favor"; KJV, "gift") of sharing in this ministry to the saints" (v. 4). Paul urged Titus in verse 6 to "complete this grace (NRSV, "generous undertaking"; RSV, "gracious work"; NIV, "act of grace") among you" (v. 6). The Greek word in all three cases is *charis*, which is normally rendered, as in 2 Corinthians 8:1, by the English word *grace*. *Grace* in these chapters is clearly something more than an abstract characteristic of an impersonal God; it has something to do with giving.

At this point we reach our chosen text. Before dealing with it, however, it would be well to consider what comes after our chosen text. There follows a section of the letter (8:16–9:5) that we might be tempted to consider merely practical or administrative in nature. Paul seems merely to be making arrangements for "administering this generous undertaking" (8:19). Once again, however, the word behind "generous undertaking" is grace. We may be tempted to think of grace as an abstract and heavenly reality. Paul seems to think that grace can become so earthly a reality, it can even be administered. In the end, says Paul, if the Corinthians carry through their undertaking, there will be hymns of praise to God because of the "surpassing grace of God" given to the Corinthians (9:14). Paul even joins in that hymn: "Thanks be to God for his indescribable gift!" (9:15). In fact, the translation once again obscures grace. Actually Paul writes, in a very strange formulation, "Grace be to God." It is as if grace overflows in the lives of those who live generously and reaches back to whence it came, to the very presence of God.

VERSES 7-8, THE GENUINENESS OF LOVE

According to Paul, the Corinthians excel in various ways. They excel, for example, "in faith, in speech, in knowledge." There may be some degree of irony in Paul's words. It appears from the correspondence as a whole that the Corinthians valued faith, speech, and knowledge to an unhealthy degree. We cannot read these words without thinking back to 1 Corinthians 13:1-2: "If I speak in the tongues of mortals and of angels . . . and understand . . . all knowledge . . . and . . . have all faith, so as to remove mountains, but do not have love, I am nothing." The offering for the poor in Jerusalem is a practical outworking of love, the "more excellent way" that Paul commends above all to the Christians in Corinth. Their love, as demonstrated by their financial generosity, must be as great as their faith, speech, and knowledge. It must also be as great as their "eagerness." Though there may have been some irony in Paul's testimony to the Corinthians' abundant faith, speech, and knowledge, there is none in the reference to "eagerness." Eagerness or zeal is precisely that quality the Corinthians display as a result of their reconciliation to Paul (2 Cor. 7:11-12).

The Corinthians also excel in love. There is a textual difficulty here, which makes the direction of the love unclear. Some manuscripts, among them those often considered the most reliable, read "our love for you"; others read "your love for us." The distinction scarcely matters for preaching purposes. Paul is appealing to the Corinthians on the basis of a newly restored love between himself and the church. This should not surprise us; the success of financial appeals, whether ancient or modern, will most likely depend on the depth of the relationship between those who ask and those who give. Where there is little love between preacher and congregation, even the best stewardship sermon will likely lead to light offering plates.

Having laid the groundwork for his appeal, Paul now says what he wants from the Corinthians: "We want you to excel also in this generous undertaking." In short, he wants them to give generously. That is an insufficiently theological statement, however. The Greek word rendered "generous undertaking" by the NRSV is *charis,* or *grace,* the third instance of the word in the chapter. The NRSV translation is inadequate. By contrast, both the RSV—"this gracious work"—and the NIV—"the grace of giving"—manage at least to retain a connection to the theological concept. It appears that most modern translators choose not to use the English word *grace* in these verses in which the reference is to a human action. Nevertheless, we may not forget that Paul actually wrote *charis,* grace. The desire to give, the ability to give, and the gift itself are intimately related to and derived from the divine grace. Paul will shortly make that connection clear in one of the most beautiful and profound statements in any of his letters.

Paul does not wish to make the appeal a command, a reluctance he will also display in the letter to Philemon.[5] Grace does not flourish in an atmosphere of obligation. The appeal is, however, inescapably a test of the genuineness of the love of the Corinthians. It is not clear from this verse whether the love Paul has in mind is love for the saints in Jerusalem, love for Paul himself as in the preceding verse, or love for God. The following verse makes the latter understanding the most likely. Surely there is a "bottom line" in our love for God. A minister in my home city once spoke this prayer at the dedication of the Sunday offering: "Lord, whatever we say with our lips, this is what we really think of you. Amen." If love has a visible bottom line, it can be measured against the "earnestness of others," a further reference to the Macedonians, Paul's standard of comparison. At this point, however, Paul offers a different and far higher standard of comparison.

VERSE 9, THE GRACE OF THE LORD JESUS

Part of Paul's general rhetorical strategy appears to remind his readers of the things they already know.[6] More specific, he reminds them of Jesus. The Corinthians cannot behave decently and in good order at communion, so Paul responds: "For I received from the Lord what I also handed on to you, that the Lord Jesus on the night when he was betrayed" (1 Cor. 11:23). They are uncertain about the resurrection: "Now I would remind you, brothers and sisters, of the good news that I proclaimed to you . . . that Christ died for our sins . . . that he was raised on the third day" (1 Cor.

15:1, 3, 4). Euodia and Syntyche are disrupting the church in Philippi: "Let the same mind be in you that was in Christ Jesus" (Phil. 2:5). Sometimes only a brief reference to the story of Jesus is necessary. How can we be sure that we genuinely have peace with God? "But God proves his love for us in that while we still were sinners Christ died for us" (Rom. 5:8).

The correspondence to the Corinthians predates the writing of our Gospels. It is therefore impossible to know how much of the story of Jesus they actually knew. There can be little doubt, however, that from the beginning of Christian history, the story of Jesus has been the church's constitutive story. A constitutive story gives identity to a group of people. Imagine a funeral of a family matriarch. After the funeral, the family gets together, shares food and drink, and rehearses the old familiar stories. In the profoundest sense, it is not the shared DNA that makes those people a family; it is the shared story. The story of Jesus and his love functions in that manner for the Christian church. It is the story we tell one another when we get together to eat and drink as "church." Indeed, the word *church* may itself be a reminder of that story; it may come from the Greek *kyriakou*, "of the Lord." (Think of the Scots *kirk* or the German *Kirche* and the connection may be clearer.) A constitutive story does more than give identity, however. It shapes all those behaviors that flow from and manifest our identity.

A constitutive story, when it is functioning properly, is so well known that only a few words are necessary to call to mind the story as a whole. So it is here. Paul does not need to tell the whole story. He need only allude to it: "You know the generous act of our Lord Jesus Christ." Once again the NRSV has obscured the presence of grace in our text. Paul writes: "You know the *charis*, the *grace* of our Lord Jesus." The grace of the Lord Jesus serves as the model for all Christian giving and indeed all Christian living.

The story of Jesus could be viewed through a variety of lenses. Here Paul understands the life of Jesus as an interchange: "Though he was rich, yet for your sakes he became poor, so that by his poverty you might become rich." How this applies to the present appeal is obvious. In the end, the chief motivation for any truly Christian giving is neither emulation of nor rivalry with others. It is not even in the first place a matter of a close and loving relationship with the one who asks. The basis for Christian giving and, indeed, all of Christian life is the gracious love of Jesus. It's all about Jesus.

Verses 10-12, Paul's Advice

According to Paul, the Corinthians were not only the first to give, but also the first even to think of giving. It is more important to finish a good work, however, than merely to begin it. Paul's impatience seems barely restrained at this point. This part of the appeal might be summarized simply: "For Christ's sake, get on with it." We might also be able to deduce one of the excuses of the Corinthian church for not finishing the project. They might be pleading poverty. (That may be why Paul brings up the Macedonians and their poverty earlier in the chapter. The apostle is determined to leave the Corinthians no excuse.) Paul is quite blunt in response to any plea of poverty. A gift is made acceptable by the willing spirit and is judged by what one has, not by what one does not have. All this is almost painfully familiar to any priest, minister, or member of a stewardship committee.

VERSES 13-15, A FAIR BALANCE

Paul also wants to prevent what would be a willful misunderstanding of the appeal. He does not intend to enrich the saints in Jerusalem by impoverishing the Corinthians, "relief for others and pressure for you." An excessively literal reading of Paul's words about Jesus could give just that idea. A foolish reader or listener might understand Paul's message as: "Just as Jesus became poor for you, so I want you to become poor for the sake of the saints in Jerusalem." Paul makes things crystal clear; he wants only a "fair balance." The surplus of Corinth and the shortage of Jerusalem ought to "balance out." The key Greek word could easily be rendered *equality*. In light of the generosity and grace of Jesus, huge discrepancies of wealth and opportunity are simply unacceptable. Grace is free, but it is never cheap. It always has consequences. One of these consequences, one might suppose from these verses, is a commitment to a "fair balance" or, more bluntly, to equality. We in our churches might sing "Amazing Grace" with delight, but this commitment to genuine equality remains a hard lesson for us to learn and harder still to put into practice.

CONCLUSION: PREACHING GRACE FROM 2 CORINTHIANS 8

The temptation for the preacher is to turn a sermon on this text into a tedious moralizing harangue, perhaps of the subcategory widely known as the stewardship sermon. It is not my intention to denigrate stewardship sermons, which are, of course, absolutely necessary. Moreover, grace always has a consequence, and very often that consequence will be financial. It is possible, however, to preach even a stewardship sermon gracefully. Furthermore, the text is a truly rich one. It need not be preached only on Sundays when the church is trying to raise money for the contemporary equivalent of the poor in Jerusalem. It could be preached on any day on which grace and the obligation of faithful living intersect, that is to say, just about any Sunday one could imagine.

On such a Sunday, the preacher's task would be to say: "For Christ's sake, get on with it." That is a possible title for the sermon. Before telling people to get on with it, however, it is vital to ensure that they remember that the whole business of getting on with it is indeed "for Christ's sake." (The shorter phrase might also be the title of a sermon.) We must not ask our listeners to give, whether it is their money, their time, or even simply their concern, if we have not also spoken with gospel warmth of the one who, though he was rich, for our sake became poor. At this point we would do well to imitate Paul. The heart of specifically Christian preaching may be to remind listeners of that which they ought already know, "the grace of our Lord Jesus." (If they do not know that grace, all the greater reason for preaching it.) A sermon on this text might therefore also be entitled, "You Know."[7]

A sermon that is faithful to the whole of this text will have two key movements, grace and demand. Theologically, grace always precedes demand. In preaching, however, it is not always necessary to say the most important thing first. Sometimes it is most effective to save the key word for the end of the sermon. The key word in this text, the word that simply must be preached if we are to be faithful to it, is *grace.* But grace need not be named early in the sermon. Grace can either be the foundation of the sermon or its climax. The sermon might move from what Paul wants the Corinthians (and us) to do to why he wants them (and us) to do it, in other words, from demand to grace. The order might be reversed; we might name the grace first and then the consequences of that grace, that is to say, move from grace to demand. Either movement would be faithful to the text. The one fatal homiletical error would be to leave out grace and preach demand only.

Because his life has been shaped by the story "of Jesus and his love," Paul lives in a world suffused with grace, a grace that flows through the most mundane and practical details of life. This grace makes even our finances a part of a universal hymn of praise. He asks the troubled and fractious Corinthians, and us, to share in that grace.

CHAPTER 2

A Word to Philemon: Grace to You and Peace

The word *grace* appears in many different contexts in Paul. The most characteristic, frequent, and perhaps significant usage may be in verses we pass over without notice. Paul greets people with the word *grace*. When Paul says hello, he always uses this word. Here are his words of greeting as they appear in the NRSV:

> Romans: "Grace to you and peace from God our Father and the Lord Jesus Christ."
> 1 and 2 Corinthians: As above.
> Galatians: Paul is furious with the Galatians but still, once again, "Grace to you and peace from God our Father and the Lord Jesus Christ."
> Philippians: Once again the characteristic greeting.
> 1 Thessalonians: "Grace to you and peace from God our Father." Perhaps Paul is in a hurry this time.
> But 2 Thessalonians goes back to the full greeting, "Grace to you and peace from God our Father and the Lord Jesus Christ."

Even in those letters widely considered Deutero-Pauline, we hear a similar greeting:

> Ephesians: "Grace to you and peace from God our Father and the Lord Jesus Christ."

A slight variation appears in Colossians: "Grace to you and peace from God our Father."

1 and 2 Timothy are a little longer: "Grace, mercy, and peace from God the Father and Christ Jesus our Lord."

Titus is only slightly different: "Grace and peace from God the Father and Christ Jesus our Savior."

And last, the little personal letter to Philemon has the familiar words: "Grace to you and peace from God our Father and the Lord Jesus Christ."

The apostle also says good-bye with the word *grace*. I will not strain the reader's patience with all the examples. But this good-bye from 2 Corinthians may be familiar: "The grace of the Lord Jesus Christ, the love of God, and the communion of the Holy Spirit be with all of you." Grace is very nearly Paul's first word and last word to the churches. And so it is with Philemon. The farewell is simpler here, but the familiar word appears: "Grace of the Lord Jesus Christ be with your spirit."

Every letter of Paul is framed with the word *grace*. It might therefore be possible to understand everything within a letter from Paul as somehow connected to the idea of grace. It would, of course, be impossible to comment here on one of Paul's longer letters. It might be possible even in a relatively short span, however, to attempt to understand the shortest of all Paul's epistles, Philemon, as a practical outworking of Paul's understanding of grace. As we shall see, it is very difficult on a specific level to determine what Paul is asking of Philemon in this letter. But on a theological level we can be more definite: Paul is asking Philemon to behave with grace toward Onesimus. To trace the outlines of grace as it manifests itself in a very complex situation is our task in this chapter.

THE STORY BEHIND PHILEMON

New Testament scholars speak of the setting, circumstances, or background to the epistle, but preachers instinctively sense that behind the epistle is a story. It is the possibility of such a story that makes preaching on this small letter inviting. And indeed, the traditional interpretation of the letter has been simple, dramatic, and compelling.

A slave, Onesimus, has fled his master, Philemon, a Christian well known to Paul (v. 15), possibly financing his flight by theft (vv. 18-19). Onesimus in some way met Paul during the latter's captivity and was converted to Christianity by him, becoming, in this sense, Paul's child (v. 10). Onesimus then became "useful," the meaning of his name, to Paul during his imprisonment (vv. 12-13). But Paul feels compelled to send the runaway back to Philemon. A recaptured slave or, for that matter, a slave who has offended his or her owner could expect severe punishment, but Paul is determined that this must not be the case with Onesimus. With careful tact and diplomacy he writes the epistle to Philemon, urging him to receive Onesimus not as a slave, but as a brother both in the flesh and in the Lord (v. 16). Indeed, Paul asks Philemon to receive Onesimus as he would receive Paul himself.

This is the story as it has been told for centuries. There are at least three other theories and, hence, stories about the origin of Philemon. According to one, held by a number of excellent New Testament scholars, Onesimus is not a runaway at all, but has gone to his master's valued friend, Paul, asking him to intercede in a difficulty between himself and his master, Philemon.[1] According to another theory, Philemon's church has sent Onesimus to assist Paul in prison, and Paul is writing to Philemon to ask him to send Onesimus back for good.[2] This would be somewhat similar to the situation behind Philippians. According to yet another scholar, Onesimus is not a slave at all, but actually Philemon's brother.[3] In the end, the least strained reading of the text remains, in my opinion, the story of a runaway slave returning to an angry master. The runaway slave story remains an inference, but it seems to me the most likely of the various hypotheses proposed to this point. For now, at least, "that's the story and I'm sticking to it!"

It is now time to turn to the letter and to look for grace in light of this story of a runaway slave returning to his master. There are many ways to read a text and many different questions can be put to it. Here I intend to read this text with a simple question in mind: "What happens when Paul's gospel of grace comes up against a more than thorny social and personal dilemma?"

VERSES 1-3, THE GREETING

Paul begins this letter, as he always does, with a greeting to those he is writing. As usual he first identifies himself. The letter is from "Paul, a prisoner of Christ Jesus." The overarching relationship here is with Jesus Christ. But the appeal to Philemon does not rest only on a "personal relationship with Jesus Christ." Grace does not lead to a "walk in the garden alone" sort of spiritual life. Being in Christ inevitably connects us to many others. Paul therefore attempts to set the story within a web of relationships. So even a partly private and individual letter does not come from Paul alone; the letter is also from "Timothy our brother." The letter is to Philemon "our dear friend [literally *agapeto*, beloved] and co-worker." But it is also to "Apphia our sister, to Archippus our fellow soldier, and to the church in your house." Apphia and Archippus may be leaders in the church or they may simply be Philemon's wife and son. (The two possibilities are not mutually exclusive.) The descriptions remind Philemon that neither he nor Paul is alone; they live within a web of Christian affiliation. The church is made up of brothers and sisters, coworkers, and fellow soldiers. Above all, in it people are "beloved." On this fundamental understanding Paul will call again and again in the letter. (See especially the heart of the letter, Paul's plea on behalf of Onesimus in verse 16.)

It is to these people that Paul writes, "Grace to you and peace from God our father and the Lord Jesus Christ." Grace is the divine favor that links us to God as father and to the Lord Jesus. It also creates a new reality in which close and loving relationships with other people are possible. The relationships that matter to Paul and ought to matter to Philemon are not "in the flesh," nor are they those created by society, but those created by that grace.

The word *grace* in a greeting is part of a pattern in Paul, but it is not a pattern he uncritically absorbed from his society. The common greeting in a letter was *chaire,* literally "rejoice." (I doubt people remembered the meaning of the word any more than contemporary people remember when they hang up the phone that our word *good-bye* really means "God be with you.") Grace, *charis,* sounds like and is etymologically related to the verb *rejoice.* But this word was not written unthinkingly. Somebody, probably Paul, quite deliberately altered the common greeting and infused it with theological meaning.

Paul also invariably combined *grace* and *peace* in his salutations. Perhaps this is because *shalom* may already have been the standard Jewish greeting that corresponded to the Hellenistic *chaire.* The two concepts also appear in the time-honored Aaronic benediction, "The LORD be gracious to you . . . and give you peace" (Num. 6:25-26). The linking of the two words reminds us that the divine favor does not exist apart from, and issues in, that wholeness in relationships that is peace.

VERSES 4-7, PAUL'S PRAYER OF THANKSGIVING

Paul then gives thanks for Philemon. (The word *you* is singular here and throughout the epistle until the final greeting.) Such a thanksgiving for those to whom Paul is writing is an almost invariable feature of Paul's letters. Once again we see relationship language, with respect both to God and to other Christians. Philemon is known for "love for all the saints and . . . faith toward the Lord Jesus." Paul prays that Philemon's "sharing of [the] faith may become effective" and acknowledges that he has received "much joy and encouragement" from Philemon's love. Moreover, "the saints have been refreshed" through Philemon. Paul is not simply following Benjamin Disraeli's advice here: "When flattering, lay it on with a trowel." Nor is he even simply advancing his case by "stressing those of Philemon's qualities upon which its outcome depends."[4] He is continuing a strategy of connecting all he says to the relationships of grace.

Verses 8-22, the Appeal

It is no surprise that when Paul moves to his direct appeal for Onesimus, he continues to use relational terms. Paul also attempts, not always with success, to exert his authority only in a way that befits this grace-shaped web of relationships. Once again we may return to the beginning of the letter. Paul normally identifies himself as an apostle.[5] In this letter, however, he seems to avoid language that might carry a straightforward claim to authority over Philemon. He appeals to Philemon not primarily as an apostle, but as "an old man" and as "a prisoner of Christ Jesus." This is a multilayered description. André Resner has argued that Paul uses "reverse ethos" in his letters.[6] That is to say, Paul ought to be considered trustworthy not because he is powerful according to the standards of the world, but because his life is conformed to the cross of Jesus Christ. Perhaps this is a "reverse ethos" assertion of authority. That Paul is a prisoner, "in chains," surely constitutes a deeply emotional appeal to Philemon and may perhaps express Paul's solidarity with Onesimus who may well end up in chains if the letter is not heeded. Such a self-designation seems to lead naturally to Paul's words, "I would rather appeal to you on the basis of love," and "I preferred to do nothing without your consent, in order that your good deed might be voluntary and not something forced." In short, the authority of the appeal lies in the nature of the relationship among Paul, Philemon, and Christ Jesus.

Paul also consciously uses relational language with respect to Onesimus. He is Paul's "child," and Paul has become his "father." As a result of this newborn relationship, the one who was formerly "useless" has become truly "useful" to Paul and potentially to Philemon. (There is a play here on the name Onesimus, which means "useful.") Indeed Onesimus is Paul's own "heart." (The Greek is actually "bowels," the seat of the emotions. The NRSV is doubtless wise in using *heart* as an emotional rather than an anatomical equivalent.) Paul strongly wished to keep Onesimus with him in Philemon's place, another appeal to the closeness of the relationships involved. Paul here reminds Philemon that Philemon himself would serve Paul if he could and that Onesimus has taken his place. The implication is clear: "If you would be willing to serve me in that manner, serve me in this: be gracious to my child."

Paul is, of course, forced to acknowledge the circumstances that have led to his present plea. Onesimus "was separated from [Philemon] for a while." If the traditional story is correct, this is a tactful paraphrase of what actually happened. In this connection it might be noted that there may have been a cause of offense other than the mere flight from slavery. Onesimus might have financed his flight by theft from his master. There was in that period an unsavory group of people called *fugitivarii.* These were in theory slave catchers, but, in fact, many of them were quite willing to smuggle runaway slaves—for a price, of course—to a big city in which it was unlikely that they would ever be found. In any case, Paul offers to pay back anything Onesimus might owe.

Philemon is to receive Onesimus back "no longer as a slave but more than a slave, a beloved brother . . . both in the flesh and in the Lord." What looks like an intrusion into the verse, the words "especially to me but how much more to you," can be understood as continuation of Paul's strategy. The relationship involved is not simply Philemon-Onesimus; it is always far more.[7] In such a web of relationships, Onesimus can be something more than "a brother after the flesh."

Both Jews and Stoics knew that slaves were brothers after the flesh to their master. To the Jews, a Hebrew slave as a member of the people of God remained a brother, and Stoics emphasized the common physical descent of all humanity. Slaves should therefore be treated with kindness. Paul is clearly aiming at something deeper than kindness here, though it is very difficult to speak more precisely about his aims. But the primacy of Christian relationship cannot be missed. It is only within such a relationship that Paul can say, "Welcome him as you would welcome me."

We have seen that Paul attempts to appeal to Philemon not as an apostle, but as an old man and a prisoner. It might appear on first reading that Paul is laying aside his much-valued authority as an apostle. He also claims, however, to be "bold enough in Christ to command you to do your duty." He can be confident of Philemon's "obedience" and can even—not very subtly—remind Philemon how much he owes Paul. As many scholars have noted, Paul appears to be pulling rank, while pretending not to do so. It does seem that he is behaving at this point more like a traditional Roman patron than a prisoner for Christ. One can hardly help speculating here. Perhaps an apostle who had spent so much of his life defending himself against assaults on his apostolic authority simply could not break old habits. Perhaps he is so desperate that Philemon should receive Onesimus back warmly that he adopts any means that will help him achieve his ends. After all, the whole business is an enormous risk, especially for Onesimus. Or it may be that Paul calculates that this is the most effective way of getting what he wants. All that may be true, but something more must be said. There is a paradoxical yet real authority that belongs to an apostle, even to one who languishes in chains. Second Corinthians 5 may give us the pattern: Paul writes as one without authority yet bearing Christ's authority.

In fact, one wonders in light of later Christian history whether Paul ought to have exerted his authority more firmly. Here and at 1 Corinthians 7:23 and Galatians 3:28, he seems so close to the realization that any form of slavery is incompatible with the fullness of the gospel of Jesus Christ. We were indeed bought with a price. How then can any one of us enslave another? In this light it is entirely understandable that Paul did not speak of his protégé's penitence or beg forgiveness. Very likely Paul did not believe escaping from slavery was a matter that required penitence and forgiveness. Paul obviously thought it best for all Christians to remain in the life situation to which they had been converted because the parousia was at hand. But he knew that Onesimus didn't really belong to Philemon. Most certainly, Paul knew who had procured Onesimus's forgiveness already. And with respect to "what is owed," Paul will pay it himself.

The fact remains, however, Paul did not explicitly condemn slavery. It is incontrovertibly true that Paul expected the second coming to wipe away all social arrangements of the old order within his own lifetime. It is also undeniable that there were in his day no democratic means, or indeed any other means, of opposing slavery. But given the tragic and shameful history of Christian involvement in the African slave trade, one can only ask wistfully, "What if?"

Paul never said to Philemon, "Slavery is wrong and less than Christian." For that matter, he did not even tell him to free Onesimus. In fact—and this is the central conundrum of the letter—he does not ask Philemon to do anything specific about him at all. This can be overstated. What Paul wants Philemon *not* to do is pretty clear. The range of possible punishments of a recaptured slave in those times was horrifying. A runaway slave might be demoted from easy to hard duty, whipped, branded, tortured, or sold into harder captivity such as the notorious salt mines that remain a byword to the present day. Even execution was possible, by crucifixion or, according to one story, by being thrown into a pool of "man-eating lampreys." But there must be no torture, salt mines, or man-eating lampreys for Onesimus. Though all that is true, we still cannot say precisely what Paul is asking Philemon to do.

It has been argued that "politeness theory" means that Paul could only word his requests indirectly and vaguely.[8] But Paul does not mince words elsewhere in his letters. John M. Barclay is far more likely to be right when he says that Paul is vague because *he did not know what to recommend.*[9] As Barclay shows, any specific course of action was fraught with difficulties. How would other Christian slaves who had done their duty feel if a runaway and a thief had been freed while they were left in slavery? (Probably like the older brother of Jesus' parable or the workers who had spent all day in the vineyard.) And if Philemon and others like him freed all their Christian slaves, would this not be an open invitation to mass conversions for understandable but less than spiritually genuine reasons? On the other hand, how can Philemon keep Onesimus in slavery and yet treat him like a brother in Christ? A brother in Christ might have the duty of reproving his master for wrongdoing! "Welcome him as you would welcome me," says Paul, but Paul certainly knew how to reprove wrongdoing. It can get tricky when preachers are forced to be specific about the consequences of grace. So Paul reminds Philemon of grace and of the web of relationships within which grace is found—and leaves him to work out the specifics for himself: "I am writing to you, knowing that you will do even more than I say."

Then the appeal concludes with a final touching request: Paul asks Philemon to get a guest room ready for him. It is yet another reminder that Paul wants the present issue to be dealt with in the context of an ongoing cordial relationship. "Refresh my heart [bowels] in Christ" (cf. v. 7). Philemon can do so in two ways: by dealing graciously with Paul's heart, Onesimus, and by continuing the relationship of warm hospitality.

VERSES 23-25, FINAL WORDS

How else would Paul end his letter? He once again links Philemon to a web of relationships, to "Epaphras, my fellow prisoner in Christ Jesus" and to "Mark, Aristarchus, Demas, and Luke." And then there appears a characteristic last word: "The grace of the Lord Jesus Christ be with your spirit."

CONCLUSION: PREACHING GRACE FROM PHILEMON

The preaching possibilities in this are surprisingly large for so small a letter. In the first place, we may learn from Philemon that grace is more than a merely personal or individual reality. Grace is inevitably understood individualistically in our individualistic culture: "Amazing grace, how sweet the sound, that saved a wretch like *me*." But grace is also that divine favor that creates and still preserves the cosmos and all that is in it and also creates and strengthens the church. Grace creates the web of relationships in which our salvation is worked out. One may therefore rightly think about grace in connection with more than the salvation of the individual person.

It remains true in our time that Christians will almost invariably experience grace within a web of relationships. Christian churches might profitably understand themselves as a counterculture of grace-enhancing relationships. As we seek our way amidst the confusions and challenges of our lives, we can at least ask, "What actions and attitudes strengthen the Christian relationships in which we live?" Furthermore, Christian leaders in a post-Christendom age will probably still have to lead—and to preach—as Paul did in Philemon, as those without authority yet having authority. It also remains likely that anyone who, like Paul, actually wants to live by grace will have to be ready to pay the debts of others, cash money.

Moreover, knowing grace does not mean we know the answers to the world's problems. Whatever grace is, it is no magic wand that waves into nothingness the perplexities of life. This is true whether we are speaking of either the great social issues of our time, the equivalents of slavery, or personal and familial issues. As a preacher and as a citizen, I often find myself baffled by the complexities of our social issues. It is almost a relief to know that Paul might not have known all the answers either, but struggled to do the best he could in a perplexing situation. In perplexity, we can sometimes only cling to and, for that matter, preach what we already know. We do know something about grace.

At this point, however, we must go beyond the letter to Philemon. Paul himself was not able to envision "this present age" without slavery. But John Barclay is certainly correct when he notes, "We must be grateful for those who in very different circumstances where social change could be both imagined and effected, dared to draw theological and practical conclusions quite beyond the reach of Paul."[10] There are times when, despite the complications, a new vision is possible. Although a particular sermon can remain with Philemon, our preaching has to go beyond its twenty-five verses. We can tell other stories, stories of those who see beyond the complexities of life to new social possibilities and who act to make them real. Justice demands it. And grace may be more than justice, but it is never less.

There remains yet another preaching possibility, however. The real evidence of the power of grace in this story belongs neither to Paul nor to Philemon, but to Onesimus. Paul sent a letter, but Onesimus risked his life.[11] Paul had been changed long ago. Onesimus had been changed by the gospel recently. But would *Philemon* change? Onesimus was so sure of the power of the gospel to change lives that he bet his own life. Moreover, he did it all for one who had done him the immense wrong of keeping him in slavery. Somebody else whose story we tell gave away his life for those who had done him wrong. There is no one—not Paul the apostle in chains, not John on Patmos, not Peter, nor any of the others—whose life more fully mirrors that self-giving love. If grace-fullness is nurtured by telling stories about grace, then surely we ought to tell the story of Onesimus. In fact, if it were possible, it would be appropriate to change the name of the letter. It might well be renamed, in honor of its hero, "The Letter Concerning Onesimus."

One week, when I was working on this chapter, I had to fill in for a local preacher on an emergency basis. I decided to preach on Philemon. Toward the conclusion of the sermon, I spoke about the tremendous risk Onesimus was taking when he returned to Philemon. I asked in the sermon what still seems to me the most important question: *Did it work?* Did Paul's letter and Onesimus's gamble have an effect? Did Philemon allow grace to shape his actions? It was a small-town Presbyterian congregation, not the sort of church in which people say anything out loud during the sermon. I was very much surprised, therefore, when an elderly lady seated in the choir said aloud, "I sure hope so!" The question, of course, is not just whether grace worked in Philemon. The question is also, "Does grace work now? Does it work in our lives and in our churches." To that question I can only respond, "I sure hope so!" But God seems to believe that it is worth taking the chance that the answer is yes. Grace may be God's gamble that we can change.

We ought to return to Philemon, however. Nobody knows whether this letter actually achieved its aim, though it is hard to imagine this little letter being preserved and passed on if Philemon had sent Onesimus to the salt mines. Why treasure a failure? There is an interesting addendum, however. Fifty or more years later, Ignatius, Bishop of Antioch, a prisoner being taken to martyrdom in Rome, writes to the Church in Ephesus, a city near Philemon's Collossae:

> I have received in God's name your whole congregation in the person of Onesimus, a man of inexpressible love who is also your Bishop. I pray that you will love him in accordance with the standard set by Jesus Christ and that all of you will be like him. For blessed is he, who has graciously allowed you, worthy as you are, to have such a bishop: a man of inexpressible love.[12]

Perhaps it is not the same person. Onesimus was a reasonably common name; and if it is the same man, he must have been very old indeed. But it certainly makes a good story and we preachers love good stories. Here is how one preacher put it: "Onesimus, runaway slave, thief, converted Christian, helper, and encourager of old men in jails, becomes Onesimus, bishop of Ephesus, yet still the helper and encourager of old men in jails."[13]

It would be amazing if it were true, but then . . .

CHAPTER 3

Ephesians 2:1-10:
By Grace You Are Saved, Through Faith

Questions that have preoccupied historical-critical interpreters are not always significant for preaching. With respect to any text in Ephesians, however, the preacher must provisionally answer a well-known historical-critical question: "Who wrote this letter?" In this case, not to give an explicit answer is to impose an implicit one. Conservative and evangelical scholars and a few others who cannot be so labeled maintain that the author of the letter to the Ephesians was, as the text asserts, the apostle Paul. Most other scholars consider it a pseudonymous writing, that is, a writing from a later generation that addresses the question "What would Paul say now?" I myself had no opinion on the subject for a number of years—until I read through the letter in Greek. To my admittedly nonexpert eye, Ephesians simply did not read like a work of the Paul of Romans, Galatians, or the other unchallenged epistles. The writing style seemed too different. This is also the fundamental argument, in a far more detailed and complex manner to be sure, of those scholars who believe Paul is not the author of the epistle. I mention this not to add to or prolong the authorship debate, but to identify for the reader the perspective from which I will be considering the text.

Certainly, the preacher ought not to denigrate or ignore the epistle on account of its authorship. Whoever may be the author of this epistle, it is as a whole a magnificent piece of early Christian theology. It found its way into the canon of the church and has nourished the theology and practice of the church ever since. Although the author is probably not Paul, he or perhaps she is a faithful interpreter of the great apostle.

Indeed, the most memorable words in our passage are a more carefully nuanced formulation concerning justification than anything we find in Paul himself.

Perhaps a personal reminiscence may be helpful here. Though I am Canadian, I was living in the United States during the bicentennial year and was even called on to preach in an American church on July 4, 1976. I remember reading at that time a newly composed essay on the state of the union written as if by Thomas Jefferson who, by an odd coincidence, had died exactly fifty years after the signing of the Declaration, on July 4, 1826. But through the medium of this sympathetic and intelligent essay, the author of the Declaration spoke once again. This foreigner, stuck with the responsibility of preaching to Americans on that special Sunday, found the essay remarkably helpful. To be preserved, the letter to the Ephesians must likewise have been truly helpful when it was written. It remains helpful to the present day.

If this epistle is indeed a writing from later in the first Christian century, it comes from a time during which the first flush of Christian enthusiasm might already have passed away. The second coming had not occurred as Paul himself had expected, and the cosmos as we know it had not been rolled up and tossed away like an old scroll. The problems of life as an ongoing church community were already apparent. There were even nominal Christians in this period who had not been active in the church for many years. In other words, the late first-century church may in some ways have been like our own.

The church to which Ephesians was written may have been very similar to the one described in a letter concerning Christians from Pliny, the Roman governor of Bithynia, a region, like the city of Ephesus, in present-day Turkey. The letter is a request for advice concerning these troublesome Christians to the Emperor Trajan. It probably stems from somewhere late in the first decade of the second century, in other words, from a time near the supposed writing of Ephesians. In passing, the letter provides some fascinating glimpses of an early Christian community, including its worship. The level of commitment of some of those accused of Christianity may sound particularly familiar:

"Others . . . at first confessed themselves Christians, and then denied it; true, they had been of that persuasion but they had quitted it, some three years [ago], others many years, and a few as [many] as twenty-five years ago."[1] The letter to the Ephesians may have been written to a church such as the one Pliny persecuted, one that may not have been, in its level of vigor and enthusiasm, very different from some of our own congregations.

Let us be very clear here: We do not decide a historical-critical question according to whether one solution "preaches better" than the other. When a particular answer yields interesting homiletical possibilities, however, the preacher is allowed to take notice. It is not only the case that the various arguments of certain historical critics are convincing, nor even that my own limited literary skills in *koine* Greek seem to corroborate their opinions. It is also that understanding this letter as a writing of a generation or so after Paul presents to us fascinating homiletical possibilities.

THE LITERARY CONTEXT

Ephesians begins in much the same manner as other Pauline or Deutero-Pauline letters, with a salutation and thanksgiving. The salutation includes the familiar words of greeting: "Grace to you and peace from God our Father and the Lord Jesus Christ" (Eph. 1:2). The thanksgiving is in the form of a traditional Jewish *berakah* or blessing (cf. 2 Cor. 1:3-4). The Greek verb here is *eulogeo*. Most of Paul's other epistolary prayers of thanksgiving begin with the characteristic Christian word *eucharisteo*. The prayer in Ephesians is considerably longer and less personal in tone than most of the other thanksgivings. Those prayers tend to thank God for some specific blessing or blessings granted to the church addressed. Here the thanksgiving is more general in tone. (It may be that the *berakah* form suits a more general form of prayer than the *eucharist* form. The prayer in 2 Corinthians is similarly general, though not nearly as long or elaborate.) But *general* is far too bland and mild a word for the thanksgiving in Ephesians. The scope of the prayer is cosmic. It stretches back to the time before time, "before the foundation of the world" (1:4), when God graciously elected us for salvation. It reaches forward toward the "fullness of time" (1:10). The coming of Christ is the turning point of this great history. The gospel of Jesus Christ has since been preached and, in the persons of the Ephesian Christians, accepted (1:13). When they believed, they were stamped with the seal of the Holy Spirit who is a pledge of the certainty of the promised inheritance. That which happens when Christians come to believe is no small thing!

In verse 15, the author then turns to the Ephesians. As in most of the epistles, there is reference to the faith of the recipients of the letter. Very quickly, however, the author returns to cosmic matters, praying that the Ephesians may be granted wisdom and vision, so they might rightly grasp what it is to which they have been called. The author piles word upon word, building up layers of praise of what God has done in Christ. The effect might be compared to entering for the first time a great Baroque church and looking up at the central dome. The breath is taken away by the gilt on the supporting pillars and by the myriad angels, prophets, and apostles in the painting on the dome, all looking toward Christ. Neither that style of architecture nor, presumably, this style of writing will appeal to everyone, but both are majestic.

If the second half of this chapter were indeed a painting, its subject would be the resurrection and its theme might be "power." In many places, Paul speaks of the cross and, by that means, the whole complex event of the death and resurrection. Here the author focuses on the resurrection itself. The immense power that raised Christ from the dead is working in those who believe. Many of the images and phrases of this part of chapter 1 will be repeated in our text. All this brings us to our text and to the question: "How do these wonders become available to us?"

VERSES 1-3, DEAD IN YOUR SINS

As we begin our passage, the author turns back once again to the Ephesians. Here, however, they are pictured not as they are in the glorious presentation of chapter 1, but as they were before they came to Christ. In that chapter, the author speaks of the Ephesians as those in whom the resurrection is now working. In the past, by contrast: "You were dead through the trespasses and sins in which you once lived." We might think here of the "before" and "after" pictures in advertisements for diet or exercise programs. These ads always portray the "before" side in all its ugliness, and so it is here.

Paul asserts in Romans that those who have come to Christ were "helpless" and even God's "enemies." The Ephesians, however, are "dead." Given the discussion of the resurrection in chapter 1, it is not surprising that the adjective *dead* describes the Ephesians "before." To be "dead" is to be estranged from the giver of life and utterly helpless. Note that the author is speaking to the Ephesians in this verse, that is, to those who are presently Christian, and hence to us as readers. The word *you* is in a highly emphatic position in the Greek text. It is as if the text were saying, "Hey you, you people who were once dead!"

The text then goes on to describe our deadness. We who hear this word were dead through our "trespasses and sins." Here "sins," appearing in parallel to "trespasses," refers to the offenses rather than to sin as a power, the usual meaning of the word in the singular. We lived in—or, more exactly, walked in—these offenses. "Walking" may be not only a more accurate translation; it may also be a more pictorial and therefore homiletically useful translation. It is as if death was for us in our pre-Christian state a way of life. The text represents not so much us choosing sin as acquiescing in it. We simply walk heedlessly along in a path determined for us by the world (literally, the "age of this world"). We walk according to the will of the "ruler of the power of the air." This ruler is a "spirit" who is at work in those who are disobedient (literally, the sons of disobedience). In an age that speaks glibly of spirituality and assumes that everything of the spirit is good, this is a sobering note. Spirituality itself can be part of this deadly path that leads away from God.

In verse 3, the author makes explicit what is already implicit by changing pronouns. No longer does the text speak of "you" but of "us." "We" lived among "them," that is, the children of disobedience, sharing their way of life. Here, the evil by which we live is not located outside ourselves in a spiritual being. Rather, it is found within ourselves. We have lived by the passions of our flesh, following the desires of our flesh and senses. *Flesh* in Paul's letters does not always refer only to our existence as bodily creatures. The word *flesh* sometimes stands for a principle within us that we might actually label spiritual, a principle of pride and resistance to the will of God. "The devices and desires" of our hearts are not merely physical. The word translated *senses* by the NRSV might be rendered *imagination*. Recent homiletics has exalted the role of the imagination in preaching. The imagination too can be enlisted in the service of the flesh, however. Nevertheless, it seems clear that the author is also speaking specifically of bodily desires at this point. This may present a serious homiletical difficulty. Some listeners may hear this text from an older dualistic frame of reference in which *spirit* is good and *flesh*, by inevitable contrast, evil. The understanding of other listeners will be shaped more by a society that all but worships the body and resists anything that appears to demean its essential goodness. Both understandings are simplistic, and neither does justice to the complexities of the text or of reality. Both sins of the spirit and trespasses of the body can be immensely harmful. And we, "like all the rest," have too easily walked that path.

This section of the text presents a number of other homiletical difficulties. The cosmology of the passage will be difficult for some listeners. We see it in language such as "ruler of the power of the air" or "spirit at work in those who are disobedient." It is not that the language itself is necessarily strange to us. "Prince of the power of the air," as the KJV renders the phrase, is a title that could easily find its place in a video game or a TV show such as *Buffy the Vampire Slayer*. (It is interesting that the mythology of evil seems to fascinate our young people. What is startlingly absent from the worlds of these games and TV shows is the reality of supernatural good. Our society is more ready to believe in Satan than in God.) It is more that most people, at least those beyond their teens, do not seem to live their daily lives as if these entities are in any way real. The prince of the power of the air is not in the frame of reference of our daily lives.[2]

One can see in these verses, however, that the author takes evil seriously. We sometimes suppose that in New Testament times everyone believed in a mythological three-story universe in which the powers of evil reside beneath us. Here, however, the ruler of this present age is pictured in the heights above us. Perhaps this is a more powerful representation of the omnipresence of evil. It resides in the very air we breathe.

Listeners may also be troubled by the negative references to "them," "children of disobedience," and "all the rest." Though the text is not exactly optimistic about the spiritual state of the "children of disobedience," the author is not inviting us to point to others and say, "Those people over there are dead!" The spiritual state of non-Christians, however negatively the author may describe it, is not the chief concern in our text. The word *dead* applies primarily *to us* as we once were.

The question is whether either the preacher or the listener is truly prepared to accept such a negative evaluation of our former spiritual state. It may be that the description will be chiefly convincing to those who have already experienced new life in Christ. It is perhaps only in light of a rich new life in Christ that the description of the former life as "dead" makes sense. This may have presented a homiletical difficulty in the original situation. It certainly presents a homiletical difficulty now. In a congregation of mixed Christian experience, there may be many for whom this description seems outdated, unconvincing, or even offensive. The solution is not to evade the text's hard word. It is to recognize that many in our society and in our churches will have trouble hearing the word and then to address the difficulty directly.

VERSES 4-8, BUT GOD . . .

At this point, the author begins one of the greatest descriptions of grace in all scripture: "But God who is rich in mercy . . . " This sounds to our ears like a doctrinal proposition. At heart, however, it is a metaphor. Due, perhaps, to the influence of this verse and similar phrases (Rom. 2:4; James 2:5), the phrase *rich in* has passed into common use in our language. As a result, the metaphor can easily be missed. The preacher might well wish to reclaim the metaphor in the sermon. At the heart of many metaphors is a picture in the imagination. Television programs such as *Lifestyles of the Rich and Famous* have given us mental pictures of fabulous and usually self-indulgent wealth. The "lifestyle" of our "rich and famous" God, by contrast, is pure mercy.

In characteristic style, the author piles description upon description: "God who is rich in mercy, out of the great love with which he loved us even when we were dead in our trespasses, made us alive together with

Christ." Several observations might be made here. In the first place, the love of God is not a newborn reality when we become Christian. The deep and passionate love of God is present for us even when we are so absent from God that we might as well be dead. God may well be a "God of the living and not of the dead," but God loves the spiritually dead too. Note the way in which the death and resurrection language of the first part of the epistle is repeated in these verses. We were dead through our trespasses (cf. 2:1). It should be noted that these trespasses are offenses against *God*. It would be natural and understandable if these offenses produced in God anger against us as "children of wrath." That is not the case, however. We have been "made alive together with Christ" (cf. 1:19-20). There then occurs a magnificent aside—"by grace you have been saved"—words that anticipate the climax of our passage. It is clear that "love" and "mercy" are not the names of two different realities. Rather, they are two ways of describing the same superlative truth. Because God's love flows not only toward those whom it would be natural for humans to love, but also to those who are "dead in their trespasses," it may also be named "mercy." To this we may now add that "grace" is not a separate reality either. Grace, it is clear, flows from and issues in the mercy and love of God. Wherever we see the mercy and love of God in scripture, there we are also seeing grace.

The author then returns to the flow of the argument and, once again, to the cosmic grandeur of the first chapter. Having been made alive with Christ, we are "seated with him in heavenly places" (cf. 1:20). One might think here either of a banquet or a throne room. The difference is not significant. What matters is that in the great painting of the exalted Christ on the dome of our baroque church, there are now other figures. Almost unbelievably, they are our own. We preachers ought to let ourselves go a little bit at this point. It is time for the "catch fire, go higher" of the African American preaching tradition. There with the glorious Christ is the gentle woman who teaches Sunday school to that difficult and inattentive class of ten- and eleven-year-old boys; there is the old man who putters around the church changing lightbulbs when he isn't swinging a hammer for Habitat for Humanity. There by the strange mercy of Christ are many whom we might not expect to see, perhaps even those ten- and eleven-year-old boys. There might, by the purest of grace, even be a clerical figure or two, those of us who try and, of necessity, fail to sketch in words the magnificence of the vision. If God's grace can reach the preacher, it can reach anybody.

Nor is this a temporary state of affairs. It will endure into "the ages to come" (cf. 1:21). In some biblical texts, the purpose of eternity is that we might praise God in an eternal "Hallelujah" chorus. Here, by contrast, the purpose is that God might continue to show us "the immeasurable riches of his grace in kindness toward us in Christ Jesus." "When we've been there ten thousand years," we will not even have begun to exhaust the richness of that grace. Once again we see the metaphor of riches in this verse. (The author employs the noun in Greek, whereas in verse 4, the related adjective appears.) Here the richness is found in grace rather than in mercy. This is yet another indication that grace and mercy are nearly synonyms. We might also notice in this verse another word that is almost a synonym for grace, namely *kindness* (cf. Rom. 2:4).[3]

There then follows the most classic and complete statement of the role of the grace of God in our salvation: "For by grace you have been saved through faith." This one line contains some of the greatest words in the biblical vocabulary. One of those words is the subject of a familiar question, "Are you saved?" The full and correct biblical answer is, "I have been saved. I am being saved, and I will be saved." The words *save, saved,* and *salvation* have a past, present, and future aspect.[4] Being saved is a process that has begun for the Ephesians at a point in the past, indeed, before the foundation of the world, and has consequences that will continue into the ages to come. All that has come before in the epistle tells us what it means to be saved. Those who have been saved are those who have been made alive with Christ and who share the glorious hope expressed in these verses. We are saved by grace through faith. It is a gift from God, "not the result of works, so that no one may boast."

Salvation, says the author, is neither our doing, nor "the result of works." A "work" in this context is anything of our own achieving of which we might boast. It is anything that we have done in which we place our trust. Our own good works cannot save us.[5] Salvation does not come from our efforts; it is a pure gift from God. This gift becomes real for us "through faith." Faith is a turning away from dependence on anything good and praiseworthy in our own selves. It is a turning to and utter dependence upon the grace of God. As a result, we cannot "boast." To boast would be to hold up some achievement or claim of our own before God and our neighbor and say, "Mine! See what I am and what I have done!"

All this reminds us forcibly of the epistles to the Romans and Galatians, with their emphasis on the doctrine of justification by faith. This is a more nuanced and complete treatment of the theme, however. Faith may never be separated from grace. The grace of God made known in the death and resurrection of Jesus Christ is the object of our faith. Saving faith is trust in God's grace. To paraphrase John Calvin writing on this text, "Faith brings people empty to God, that they may be filled with the blessings of Christ."[6] Faith opens us to grace.

Good works are not, however, irrelevant. "We are what God has made us, created in Christ Jesus" (cf. Gal. 3:28). The purpose of this second Genesis is to do good works. We may not take credit even for these good works, however. These works have been prepared beforehand. In a magnificent phrase, the author reminds us that these good works are to be our way of life. This and no other is "the Christian way of life."

Conclusion: Preaching Grace from Ephesians 2

Genuinely to preach that we are saved by grace through faith and not by works forces us to face certain difficult questions. In the first place, it forces us to consider the language we use with respect to salvation. During Paul's ministry, he faced those who proclaimed "another gospel." These people supposed that the heart of the Christian faith is adherence to the law. They believed and tempted others to believe that our own good works save us. It is still entirely possible that Christians may be tempted to trust in our own good works. We might not use the language of Paul or the letter to the Ephesians and speak of being *saved* or *justified* by these good works. We might say, however, that we find a sense of self-worth and pride in our own goodness. There are some vital questions here. Is a sense of "self-worth" or of "self-esteem" really the same thing as salvation "by faith through grace"? Does preaching a gospel that abandons the language of justification by grace through faith in favor of the language of contemporary popular psychology constitute "preaching another gospel"? These are enormously important questions that the text, if allowed to speak clearly, forces upon the preacher.

The text clearly contrasts trust in God's grace and trust in our own good works, but without specifying what those "good works" might be. It must be emphasized that we are most tempted to put our trust in works that are genuinely *good.* So, for example, Christians who are committed, and very rightly so, to God's demand for justice might suppose that their true value and purpose in God's eyes lie in their social attitudes, commitments, and activities. From there, it could be a perilously easy step to a smug certainty of superiority over those with less enlightened social views. Surely this would be the equivalent of "boasting."

We might say something very similar about those of us who cling to the older language of "justification through faith." In our day, some Christians, particularly in evangelical circles, speak almost as if they have been saved by "committing their life to Christ." Let it be very clear: It is a profoundly right and holy act for any of us to commit our lives to Christ, but we must not put our trust in that commitment. There is a very great danger that in our time faith or, more exact, our expressions of faith might become in the technical sense a "work." We are not actually saved by "committing our life to Christ" or by any religious act of our own. We are saved only by the grace of God. We may not even hold up our faith in Christ before God and our neighbor and say "mine!" That, in a damnable contradiction in terms, would be to boast in our faith. If we do so, it fools only ourselves. God knows better, and our neighbors are offended by our spiritual presumption. In all this the Christian gospel itself is brought into disrepute by our arrogance. We still need to hear, "By grace you have been saved, through faith, and this is not your own doing."

Grace in the Gospels

CHAPTER 4

John 5:1-18: But Do You Want to Get Well?

A characteristic of the Gospel of John is the use of misunderstanding as a literary strategy. So Nicodemus, for example, misunderstands the word of Jesus, "You must be born again from above." This gives Jesus, and the evangelist, the opportunity to speak about the meaning of the new birth. But we ought to be warned. Misunderstanding not only is a feature of the narrative in John; it is also a possibility for the interpreter. It is terribly easy, especially in contemporary North America, to misunderstand this passage and in so doing miss the grace that is so richly there. We can see two of those realities that Christians often prefer to grace in what at first sight appears to be a straightforward healing story. It should be noted, however, that the story does not end with the healing. Rather, it leads into a controversy over the fact that the healing took place on a Sabbath. The healing itself is one of the seven "signs" of the glory of Christ of the Fourth Gospel. As such, we will expect the pericope to point in some way to the glory of Christ. This we will find: "My Father is still working, and I also am working," says Jesus. Though the word *grace* does not appear in the story, we will find that, in it, grace has everything to do with the Father's work.

THE LIMITS AND THE CONTEXT OF THE PASSAGE

With respect to many passages of Scripture, the choice of limits is a major interpretive decision. So it is with our text. It is easy to identify the beginning of our passage. Verse 1 indicates a change of both place and location, "After this there was a festival of the Jews, and Jesus went up to Jerusalem" (John 5:1). The subject matter also differs from what has gone before. The previous pericope, John 4:46-54, the healing of an official's son, is a self-contained report of a healing miracle reminiscent of the Synoptic Gospels. Our passage also reports a healing miracle, but in a way that is much more characteristic of John in that it leads directly into a lengthy discourse. This is what creates the difficulty for the careful exegete and preacher. Where to begin reading is easy; where to end is not. One could easily justify on exegetical grounds reading the entire chapter, but in most churches that is not a practical option.

The Revised Common Lectionary, for which this passage is the alternate reading for the sixth Sunday of Easter in Year C, ends the reading at verse 9, with the report of the physical healing. The framers of the lectionary tend to avoid "trouble" where possible. That is to say, they excise from the reading for the day verses or sections of the text that seem nasty or unpleasant. (Sometimes they will even cut out a half verse in the midst of a reading for this reason.) Moreover, the framers may have been concerned, rightly, with anti-Judaism in the selected readings. Cutting the text at verse 9 allows the reader to avoid the troubling interchange with the "Jews" in verses 10 and following. Even a cursory reading of the text shows, however, that this division is exegetically indefensible. The story does not end at verse 9, and, indeed, the most interesting bits of the story are at the end. As in a scorpion, the sting is in the tail.

In general, moreover, it is a serious homiletical mistake to avoid trouble in a text. Texts from which all the trouble has been strained out are about as tasty as pablum. Indeed, some homiletical theory asks the preacher to look actively for trouble in the text as a starting place for preaching. On both homiletical and exegetical grounds, the lectionary division of the text is not acceptable.

One might compare—in this and many other respects—this passage to the story of the healing of the man born blind found in John 9. There are important similarities between the two miracle stories. Both healings take place on the Sabbath. After each healing, the religious authorities interrogate the one who has been healed, though the exchange with the man born blind (and his parents) is far more extensive. As we shall see, the attitudes of those healed differ in the two narratives, but that point can be left for later. In both cases, Jesus meets the one who has been healed for a second time and addresses him. There is even mention of a pool in both narratives. Far more important is the fact that, in both complexes, Jesus discloses the nature of his own work. In chapter 9, however, the disclosure is contained in one statement pregnant with meaning, "I came into this world for judgment so that those who do not see may see, and those who do see may become blind" (John 9:38). In our passage, by contrast, the statements grow into a lengthy discourse. Chapter 9 is one integrated story, and the editors of the Revised Common Lectionary, recognizing this truth, have taken the unusual step of having the whole chapter read aloud. In chapter 5, however, there appears to be a slight break between the healing and its subsequent exchanges, on the one hand, and the discourse that follows, on the other. This validates a decision to cut the pericope after either verse 16 or 18. Verses 16 and 17 might be considered the hinge between the sign and the discourse and might rightly be assigned to either.[1]

The present narrative finds its place in a complex of discourses and "signs." Following the paired discourses with Nicodemus, a ruler in Israel, and a Samaritan woman, Jesus and the disciples return to Galilee. The description of the Galileans' reaction to Jesus is puzzling. Jesus' words— "A prophet has no honor in the prophet's own country" (John 4:44)—are quoted, but in fact, Jesus' compatriots actually appear to hold him in considerable honor. They "welcomed him, since they had seen all that he had done in Jerusalem at the festival" (John 4:45). But Jesus hardly appears to be impressed by a welcome that depends only on miracles. When a representative Galilean, a royal official, comes to him to beg for healing for his son, Jesus all but chides him, "Unless you see signs and wonders you will not believe" (John 4:48). Despite this rebuke, Jesus does heal the son by the simple exercise of his word. The healing itself seems not to be the only point of the story however. There is also a human response. The father realizes that the son has regained his health at the very moment Jesus had spoken and does believe, together with his whole household. This, of course, simply confirms Jesus' observation concerning their reason for belief. John's Jesus has a somewhat jaundiced view of faith, which is dependent only on miracles. Note that belief is here a response to the miracle, not a prerequisite for it. This point needs further discussion but can be laid aside for a moment. For the moment, all that needs to be said is that a healing is performed for the benefit of one whose motives are not wholly admirable.

Though there has intervened an unspecified passage of time and a journey to Jerusalem, our passage immediately follows this sign. This is the only place in the Gospel of John where two signs are placed side by side. Surely this placement is in itself a "sign" that we should consider the two miracles together.

VERSES 1-9A, THE HEALING

Setting the Scene: Verses 1-5

The occasion of the journey is a "festival of the Jews."[2] Though scholars have speculated as to which feast is meant here, no more specific information is given in the text. Any of the feasts were celebrations of God's great work for the children of Israel in the past. What better time for a sign that "my Father is still working"? The setting of the miracle is a pool by the Sheep Gate called Bethzatha or Bethesda. There are small textual difficulties here that are the province of a technical commentary rather than the present work. Bethesda might be preferable on technical grounds because of a reference in the writings from Qumran. It might also be more symbolically rich for American hearers because of the famous naval hospital. This pool will become a place of healing.

John specifies that the pool has five porticoes. In older interpretations, it was claimed that the five porticoes were largely symbolic, standing for the five books of the Torah. Jesus, it was argued, could give what Torah could not, namely, healing. The pool was then excavated, the five porticoes discovered, and the symbolic interpretation fell into disfavor. The number may, however, be both actual and symbolic though it need not be interpreted in an anti-Jewish fashion. The Torah and all it represents is a necessary preparation for the present work of Jesus. In the story and perhaps in life, we meet Jesus in the gates of the Torah. As Jesus has told the Samaritan woman in the previous chapter, "Salvation is from the Jews" (John 4:22).

By this pool lie many invalids, the blind, lame, and "dried up" or "withered." The text does not actually tell us why they were there. Older listeners who grew up with the King James Version of the Bible may remember an explanation.[3] It was believed that an angel stirred the waters and the first to enter the waters would be healed. This is an explanatory addition that appears in the manuscripts followed by King James's translators. These were not the oldest and most reliable manuscripts, and the verse therefore does not appear in most contemporary translations. The explanatory addition is, however, a very old one, known by Tertullian in about the year 200. It reflects an ancient tradition and something like this understanding is required to make sense of the rest of the story. (This textual difficulty is also the reason the verse numbering jumps from 3 to 5 in the NRSV. Verse 4 was the addition.)

Textual matters such as this are always a challenge to the preacher. My late father, knowing my predilection for academic details, used to say to me, "You can't footnote a sermon." To be sure, any extended treatment of this problem might well cause eyes to glaze over. On the other hand, the issue does provide an opportunity for some incidental teaching about the Bible. Perhaps a very brief reference is all that is necessary. A sermon on this text will probably require at least some retelling of the story, at least to get us to the crux of the passage. When doing so we might say, "Some ancient manuscripts of the Gospel add an explanation of why the invalids were there," and so on. Alert listeners might note the words and ask for more details later. Others would at least learn in passing that there are different manuscripts of the Bible. Lessons learned in passing are often surprisingly valuable.

Among these invalids by the pool was a man who had been ill for thirty-eight years. This is almost a full biblical generation of forty years. Perhaps the number suggests that there is almost no time left for him. It is interesting that the text does not actually specify the man's illness. Perhaps, as we shall see, his primary illness is not a disease of the body.

But Do You Want to Get Well? Verses 6-9a

The sick man is the chief actor in the story, next to Jesus, and it is to him that Jesus poses a question that to contemporary ears sounds like the key to the whole story. You can imagine the question of the church sign as the title of a sermon: "Do You Want to Be Made Well?"

To contemporary interpreters, this appears to be a tantalizing homiletical avenue into the text. "Do you want to be made well?" asks Jesus of the sick man. Perhaps the text is telling us that a vital factor in wholeness is the desire actually to be well. It is as if the key to healing is something in the man himself. It is as if the key to wellness of any sort is in our own attitudes.

There may be a good deal of truth to this notion. There is scientific evidence that a positive attitude does affect our health for the better. Wellness, it may be, is really up to us. But the fact remains that we are not well. If this is the case, perhaps Jesus is asking us, and we ought likewise to ask ourselves, "Do we really want to be made well?" The question may well be inviting, but it is by no means harmless. The question begins to have some bite to it.

In the text, the answer may be no. The man's answer as it appears in the text is, quite obviously, no real answer at all. "Sir, I have no one to put me into the pool when the water is stirred up; and while I am making my way, someone else steps down ahead of me." "Someone else . . . " We will hear similar words later in the text. It does seem a feeble answer at best. It is clear that the sick man carefully avoids giving a clear and simple positive answer. His answer is not a plain yes.

There is a commentary on the Gospel of John written by Jungian psychologist John Sanford. Sanford claims the paralytic belongs to a psychological category he calls "turtle." Turtles are people so afraid of life that they withdraw into a shell. The turtle, says Sanford, "may seek out a life-situation in which as few demands as possible are made upon him. Such a situation might be an illness. . . . He may also secretly (keeping it secret even from himself) carefully nurse his illness along so as to prevent a cure."[4] The man's a turtle. "Someone always gets there before me," complains the turtle. After all, turtles don't move very fast.

But we ought not to laugh too hard at the turtle. When we consider the great illnesses that afflict both individuals and society and when we consider how many are at least in part self-inflicted, any laughter would surely begin to ring hollow. Perhaps the truth is that we don't really want to be well either. When Jesus' question is addressed to us it begins to have some bite. After all, we know about smoking and its dreadful consequences. We know about the dangers of alcohol. Every child is told of the dangers of drugs in countless publicity campaigns. Millions of dollars are spent every year in our society promoting "safe sex." Closer to home for many of us preachers might be the whole business of a healthy diet and regular exercise. We know what will lead to health, but by and large we do not live by what we know. Jesus might well ask us, "Do you want to be made well?" We would have a hard time answering.

If we move from individual wellness to social health, the question becomes even more complicated. Social ills are far harder to cure than physical diseases, but even here we cannot plead ignorance. We know very well the corrosive effects of poverty and violence in our society, but do we actually do very much about it? We know about the sad effects of widespread family breakup. We can describe the probable consequences of living in a world with an enormous divide between poverty and wealth. It might be a very uncomfortable thing for us as a society to face Jesus' question, "Do we really want to get well?"

Is the Desire to Help Ourselves a Precondition for Grace?

"Do we really want to get well?" is an excellent diagnostic question both for the turtle and for ourselves. The difficulty is that in our present social climate, it may be much too tantalizing and seductive a question. The interpreter may be tempted to take this question and run with it, away from our text and the gospel it proclaims. The story as a whole can be misinterpreted in two different ways, both of which spring from a search for a necessary human precondition to grace. One misinterpretation is religious and the other social. The social misinterpretation will likely concentrate on this question and find in it the secular gospel of self-help. That secular gospel is so pervasive and so alluring, to the preacher as to the congregation, that at least a short treatment of the subject is necessary here.

The Greek verb translated as "want" refers to the exercise of the will. A possible translation is, "Do you will to become well?" It might appear that the key to wellness is an exercise of the will. We have to *want* to get well. We believe fervently in self-help. As a well-known "Bible" verse reminds us, "The Lord helps them who help themselves." In fact, one can spend all day with a concordance and not find that verse in the Bible. The words do reflect a core value of our society, however. Core value might even be too weak a phrase. Self-help might be, to borrow a term from Paul, "another gospel" for us.

Our society is in love with the idea. Think, for example of all the self-help books. If you read them, you'll become healthy and wealthy though probably not wise. But, why worry about wisdom when you can be happier, more fit, and much, much sexier?

> You'll *Make the Connection* to a better body (while writing it all down in your *Journal of Daily Renewal*), begin to *Eat Right for Your Type, Learn the Seven Habits of Highly Effective People,* and *Retire Wealthy in the 21st Century.*[5]

These books sell considerably better than the proverbial hotcakes. "According to the American Booksellers Association, sales of self-help books have increased every year since 1991."[6] The dominance of self-help books is remarkable. A leader in the Canadian publishing industry puts it simply, "Self-help blows fiction out of the water."[7] That is a Canadian reality, but is it likely to be very different in the land of the free and the home of the Oprah?

In this connection, it might be a good idea for the preacher to carry out an exegesis of the magazine rack at the nearest newsstand. A huge percentage of the titles will have to do with self-help. Most of the titles will tell you how to get yourself fit, lose weight, earn more money, get the most out of your computer, or have a spring/summer/fall/winter makeover. My favorite title when I tried this exercise was "Fifteen Ways to Fake Fabulous Skin!"

The gospel of self-help is proclaimed not only in books and magazines. We also hear it in the movies, from championship locker rooms, from Olympic gold medalists, from successful politicians, and from far too many pulpits. In this form, it is usually some version of "You can be anything you want to be if you dream hard enough. If you want it bad enough you can get it!" We hear it from so many sources, but it is still not true. This is closer to the truth: Olympic silver medalists and seventh-place finishers and people who don't even make the Olympic team at all work as hard and dream as hard as the gold medalist. Perhaps even more distressing is that we say these things to our children. Following our dreams is a staple of inspirational speakers at elementary school graduations. That is hardly surprising. Who would want to hear something closer to the truth on such an occasion? "Dare to dream, but be ready to adjust your dreams to reality. Work hard to achieve your dreams, and you may accomplish something remarkable; and in any case, you will almost certainly be farther ahead than if you didn't dream, and work, at all." But the school board wouldn't like that.

Self-help is not a whole lie, of course. There is something in it, just enough to make it a half-truth. Half-truths are actually more dangerous than whole lies, however, because they are more likely to be believed—and to be preached. Self-help in our society might even be called an idol. This does not mean that self-help is evil any more than it is a complete lie. In the biblical world, idols often represented a good part of creation, the sun, rain, wisdom, and so on. If people exalted this good part of creation to the point that they accorded to it some of the attributes of God, this good thing became an idol. We may be tempted to do the same. God alone can save. If we trust self-help to save us, it has become for us an idol.

Sadly, idols can be very cruel. An emphasis on self-help may serve as a justification for ignoring the needs of others. "They have to want to improve their lot in life. We can't help them if they won't help them-selves," we may intone as we pass by on the other side.

If our story were actually an early version of the gospel of self-help, one would expect the sick man to leap to his feet. We might picture him shouting, "Yes, I want to be made well, I want to throw aside all my self-defeating defense mechanisms!" The turtle would shed his shell and walk away free and changed, a man at last. Manifestly, nothing remotely like that happens. The role of the question, "Do you want to get well?" is not to give us a homiletical springboard for an exhortation to self-help. It is to show that nothing in the man himself leads to his healing. There is no textual evidence whatsoever that the man is healed, even in part, by the exercise of his own will. He never chooses health and well-being. He doesn't help himself, but Jesus helps him nevertheless. The story seems to show us that Jesus even helps those who can't or won't help themselves.

VERSES 9B-15, THE CONSEQUENCES OF THE HEALING: IS FAITH A PRECONDITION FOR GRACE?

The second potential religious misinterpretation of this text is a religious one. It would come from looking for faith in the story. We have a notion that Jesus heals in response to faith, as if faith were a precondition to grace. There are, after all, several miracle stories that suggest this. So, for example, Jesus says to the woman with the issue of blood, "Daughter, your faith has made you well" (Mark 5:34). But there is no evidence that the man in this story shows any faith whatsoever before he is healed. In fact, there is no evidence of faith in the man even *after* the healing. A comparison with John 9 is once again instructive. There the one healed makes an explicit confession of faith, "Lord, I believe" (John 9:38) and, as a consequence of his faith, is driven out by the authorities. (This is clearly a picture of the fate of Jewish Christians in the time of composition of the Gospel.) Nothing remotely like this happens in chapter 5. There is no evidence whatever that at any point the man who was healed showed faith in Jesus. Sometimes in the Gospels, faith precedes a miracle. At other times, faith may be a response to the miracle as in John 9. It may not come at all, as in our text. Grace does not depend on faith, though faith depends on grace. As Jesus puts it, God "causes the sun to shine on the righteous and the unrighteous" (Matt. 5:45).

The man does not even learn very much from the experience. The healing took place on a Sabbath day, and the "Jews" rebuked the man for violating the Sabbath by carrying his mat. (See the brief appendix to this chapter on the "Jews" in John's Gospel. I take the "Jews" here to mean the religious authorities who oppose Jesus.) He responds, "The man who made me well said to me 'Take up your mat and walk.'" In reading the lesson, this should be spoken in the same tone as "someone else steps down ahead of me." Both sentences should be read aloud with a whine. For this turtle there is always "someone else." The authorities, quite naturally, are eager to know who this troublemaker and scofflaw is, but the man cannot tell them for Jesus has disappeared into the crowd. Jesus remains the one in control of the action of the story. This little exchange with the "Jews" sets up the theologically vital conclusion to the miracle story in verses 16 through 18.

The story goes on. Jesus, as in John 9, meets the man he has healed a second time. According to the story, he is under no illusions concerning the spiritual state of the man he has healed: "See, you have been made well! Do not sin any more, so that nothing worse happens to you." Manifestly, the man does not heed Jesus or even show elementary gratitude. Once again, a contrast with John 9 is instructive. There, the healed man resists the authorities in a manner that can only be called feisty. Even his parents are feisty. Here, however, the one who has been healed actually goes so far as to inform on Jesus. Apparently the turtle resents losing his shell: "As he walked away, it seemed his soul was just as crippled as it was when we first saw him sitting like a sack of potatoes by the pool."[8] There may be a temptation at this point to turn the story into a moral lesson warning us against ingratitude. Of course, we ought to flee ingratitude. That is not, however, the most important reality in the story. The story is actually not about human gratitude or ingratitude, but about a savior who will heal even a helpless, hopeless loser and snitch.

It would seem to us justice if "something worse" did indeed happen to this man, but within our story, nothing "worse" comes to pass. The man is, in fact, able to walk away, healed physically. In theological terms, he has received grace, and it is not taken away from him. A comparison with chapter 9 shows, however, that the man has missed an even greater grace, the grace of discipleship. Nevertheless, he can walk and that is no small thing. It is tempting to wonder whether anything worse did happen later, but the Gospel gives us no information whatever. As we who have read the rest of the Gospel know, however, "something worse" does happen, but it happens to Jesus. It is not justice, but it just may be grace.

Verses 16-18, a Link to Jesus' Discourse

The pericope ends with an explicitly theological note that serves as a transition to the lengthy christological discourse that takes up the rest of the chapter. As in the Synoptic Gospels, conflict arises between the authorities and Jesus because he heals on the Sabbath. But characteristically of John, a more explicitly theological viewpoint is added: "My Father is still working, and I am also working." We can only understand this "work of God" in this context as exemplified by the story we have just read. God reaches out to heal and to save even those who are unworthy of help, even, as in this case, a snitch and informer. The story is not about faith. As we have already seen in the previous pericope, John's Jesus is actually suspicious of faith that comes only from miracles. The story is about grace. Grace is always present in the Gospel; the human response differs. In preaching grace, it is absolutely vital that we get the order right: divine initiative, human response even if that response, as in this case, is faithlessness.

Conclusion: Preaching Grace from John 5

This story makes us face the scandalous particularity of grace. Why would Jesus heal this particular man, scoundrel that he is, out of all the invalids by the pool? This kind of particularity stands against the customary standards of society. We want good things to happen to people who have deserved it. Secularists might wish good things to come to those who help themselves; religious folk might suppose that blessings ought to come to those who have faith. Both ideas are attempts, in slightly different ways, to identify the preconditions for grace.

In fact, the difference between the two approaches might be very slight indeed. We had a family friend who became seriously ill and was diagnosed with pancreatic cancer, a form of cancer with a particularly poor prognosis. He was a minister of an unusual kind, the kind of minister who is liked and respected by both liberals and conservatives in the church. His clergy friends of a liberal persuasion used to come to him in his hospital room and say, "If you keep the right mental attitude, you can beat this thing." His conservative colleagues said, "If you have enough faith, God will cure you." Both sides put the responsibility on him. His healing would come from something within him, his faith or in his positive mental attitude, a standard phrase of the self-help gospel. Different words surely, but is the tune very different? In the end, his wife had to ban both sets of friends from his bedside.

If this text offends both believers in faith and believers in self-help, to whom can we preach it? The answer, I believe, is to most of our listeners. Most of them, I suspect, have areas in their lives in which they cope well. There are parts of their lives in which they can indeed help themselves. I doubt that they will meet Jesus in those parts. There are, however, very likely to be areas of their lives in which they try and try and try again and can never seem to be or to do what they want. They cry out wordlessly for help from somewhere deep within, for they cannot help themselves. There is no point concealing the truth here. The reason I suppose that our listeners are like that is very simple: It is that way with me. There are areas in my life in which I am nothing more than a "turtle." But Jesus will even help turtles. And that, too, is grace.

EXCURSUS: PREACHING ON THE "JEWS" IN THE GOSPEL OF JOHN

Many listeners will notice a troubling reality when the text is read aloud. Here, as elsewhere in the Gospel of John, the "Jews" are the villains of the piece. "The man told the *Jews* that it was Jesus who had made him well." "Therefore the *Jews* started persecuting Jesus." If it read "the religious authorities" or "chief priests and scribes" or even the "Pharisees and Sadducees," it might be more acceptable. "Religious authorities who oppose Jesus" is what the text may well actually mean, but the text simply says the Jews.

In the post-Holocaust era, no Christian preacher with even a modicum of decency speaks negatively about the "Jews" in general, but our text and many other texts in John do so. It is true that these texts come out of a time of conflict and eventual separation between majority Judaism and the nascent Christian movement. The text is not anti-Semitic in the modern sense of the word, in other words, advocating hatred of Jews in general for racial or ethnic reasons, but historical observations of that sort do not really aid the preacher on Sunday morning. It is not possible here to deal extensively with the problem of anti-Judaism in the New Testament. I can only offer some humble advice on how to preach texts such as these.

In the first place, it seems to me that preachers ought to face trouble head-on. It is better to explain explicitly how one deals with references like these rather than to ignore them. At some point in preaching John, not necessarily with this text in which the references are not actually as harsh as in some other passages, it might be possible to say something like the following:

The text was written in a time of mounting bitterness between what was becoming mainstream Judaism and the young Christian church. In a time of anger and division, harsh words are sometimes spoken and written. So it was when the Gospel of John was written. In those days, Christians were a minority within a minority. Later, Christianity became the dominant religion of the Roman Empire and the Jews remained a minority. The hostility born in those early days endured and festered. Often it became a virulent disease with tragic and appalling consequences. In the face of that horrible history of prejudice and violence, we followers of the Rabbi from Nazareth must hang our heads in shame. We must also resolve, "Never again!"

Nevertheless, we may still use these texts from the Gospel of John and find spiritual nurture in them. We first ought to recognize that these texts in general and our text in particular were primarily written not against Jews, but for Christians. The Gospel of John was written that Christians might take warning, choose rightly, and find life. The conclusion of the first edition of the Gospel says, "These are written so that you may come to believe that Jesus is the Messiah, the Son of God, and that through believing you may have life in his name" (John 20:31). In commenting on the discourse that follows this healing in John 5, John Sanford writes:

> Though the discourse is couched in the form of a diatribe to the Jews, it is in fact intended for us, the readers. . . . By the "Jews" we mean not those who espouse the faith of Judaism, but all those people who remain so entrenched in old attitudes that they are not open to the new life of the spirit. Since we all are partly, or perhaps even largely, caught in our old psychological structures, we are the ones to whom Christ is speaking.[9]

In other words, we Christians can be the "Jews." We may be the ones who cannot recognize what God is doing, who prefer pious paralysis to Jesus' healing.

CHAPTER 5

Mark 7:24-30: Crumbs Under the Table

Perhaps I might be permitted to write this chapter a little differently and in a considerably more personal vein. Instead of offering a commentary working through a particular text, may I tell you the story of a particular sermon? We will, nevertheless, cover much the same ground as in our previous chapters of commentary.

It all began when Linda, one of my former students, asked me to preach an anniversary service at her church in rural Ontario. I was delighted to accept, partly because I have a real fondness for small churches in rural Ontario and partly because I also have a real fondness for Linda. Linda was always one student who listened intently to whatever I had to say in class or out of class. But she didn't merely accept my good advice with the reverence due Moses descending from the mountaintop, stone tablets in hand. (Like most professors of homiletics, I am a professional dispenser of good advice and prefer to have that advice received with due reverence.) Linda invariably poked and prodded and questioned. If there was a weak spot in my presentation, something I would rather pass over quickly without notice from the students, Linda invariably found it and named it out loud for all to hear. But the sting never lasted long for the simple reason that Linda was transparently committed to truth and in her questioning was paying me the enormous compliment of assuming that I was just as committed as she was. We professors are always tempted to become more wedded to our own formulations than to truth. With Linda around, it was always difficult to give in to that particular temptation and I was grateful. Besides, she was and is quite simply a likable sort of person, so I was glad to accept.

One piece of good advice I offer all my classes is this: "Consider using the lectionary." Linda, I knew, was following the lectionary, so when the time came to prepare the sermon for her church, I turned to the lectionary readings for the anniversary Sunday. To my dismay, I found that the Gospel reading for the day was Mark 7:24-37, which contains two pericopes, the dialogue between Jesus and the Syro-Phoenician woman and the healing of a deaf man in the Decapolis. The problem was that the first pericope, the dialogue with the Syro-Phoenician woman, has always been for me one of the most troubling passages in the Gospels. It isn't at first reading a cheerful text, and I knew very well that I did not want to preach it on a celebratory occasion such as an anniversary service. Moreover, it pretty clearly falls into the category of "hard text," and it is always better to preach hard texts to people with whom one has a pastoral relationship. It would be difficult to preach to people whom I did not know and who did not know me. But those were rationalizations. The real reason I did not want to preach the text was that it had always made me uncomfortable.

When speaking about the lectionary, I usually claimed that one advantage of the lectionary is that it makes us preach on the texts we don't like rather than just our pet passages. "Wrestle with the hard texts," I would say. "It's in the wrestling that you will find a blessing." I was almost certain that I had said this in Linda's hearing at one time or another. "Be sure your good advice will find you out!" says the Bible, or at least something much like that. I considered using one of the other texts for the day or concentrating on the second pericope in the Gospel lesson, but I had a sinking feeling that Linda would know exactly what I was doing—evading a hard text because it made me uncomfortable. So with genuine reluctance I turned to the story of the Syro-Phoenician woman and to its troubling picture of Jesus.

"From there he set out and went away to the region of Tyre," the text tells us. The location is important; this is Gentile country to the north of Galilee, what we now call Lebanon. "He entered a house and did not want anyone to know he was there." It sounds as if Jesus is on retreat or at least a holiday and wants to be alone. The literary context is almost always a key to preaching from Gospel texts, and so it is here.[1] When we consider the flow of narrative in the Gospel as a whole, it is easy to see why Jesus wants privacy. The "crowd" is a major character in the Gospel of Mark. From the beginning of the Gospel, Jesus has been surrounded by crowds. He has healed the sick, driven out demons, and taught with a power beyond that of the religious authorities. What happens as a result?

There are more and bigger crowds and more problems to solve. Even by the end of the first chapter of Mark's Gospel, the word about Jesus is out. As a result, "Jesus could no longer go into a town openly, but stayed out in the country; and people came to him from every quarter" (Mark 1:45). As the Gospel begins, so it continues.

Mark does not paint for us a picture of uniform success and acceptance, however. Also, from very early in the Gospel, the religious authorities are deeply suspicious of Jesus. Those same activities that draw the crowds draw official anger. Beginning at Mark 2:1, the evangelist tells us five successive stories of growing conflict with the religious leadership. By the end of those five stories, the enmity is fixed and deadly: "The Pharisees went out and immediately conspired with the Herodians against him, how to destroy him" (Mark 3:6).

This double pattern, set very early in the Gospel, is continued in the immediate literary context of our text. Once again there are miracles and, with the miracles, more crowds: Jesus feeds five thousand (Mark 6:30-44) and stills the sea (Mark 6:45-52). When he reaches the other shore, once more, the crowd appears, and he heals many (Mark 6:53-56). But there is also opposition. The Pharisees and some of the religious experts from Jerusalem challenge his disciples' behavior. The disciples, they charge, do not engage in the proper ritual washings and are therefore defiled (Mark 7:1-6). The key to this dispute is "the tradition of the elders," which accords great importance to such matters. Jesus' reply might be understood in light of a time-honored maxim of our own culture, "The best defense is a good offense." Jesus' aggressive response is twofold. In the first place, he attacks the questioners themselves, displaying for all to see their failure to live by the law they themselves claim to revere (Mark 7:8-13). It is not, however, only the case that they fail to live up to the traditions they hold in honor. The traditions themselves are flawed in that they concentrate on the wrong things. In an instruction directed not at the Pharisees themselves, but, significantly, to the crowd, Jesus declares that it is not what goes into a person that defiles but what comes out—fornication, theft, murder, and so on (Mark 7:17-23). In short, the old ways of looking at reality are no longer good enough. In an exegesis paper, we could say, "This brings us to the beginning of our pericope." In a sermon in which information is conveyed narratively, we say, "No wonder he needed a break."

At this point, a methodological point must be raised. There are differences between exegesis undertaken for publication among the guild of biblical scholars (or for a class assignment to one particular biblical scholar) and exegesis undertaken in preparation for a sermon. At least in some older forms of exegesis, it is possible and even encouraged to avoid

the explicitly theological. Most certainly the scholar eschews in the name
of proper academic objectivity any existential involvement with the text.
Exegesis for the sake of preaching, by contrast, must always seek the theological and recognize the existential.

It might be well to be even more specific. It would be anachronistic to
assume that Mark is interested in the complications that this passage
presents for what would later become orthodox Christology. Either the
traditional historical critic or the newer literary critic might rightly ignore
these matters. For the one preparing to preach in a church shaped by that
Christology, however, such considerations are proper and indeed
inevitable.[2]

It is right, therefore, to name an existential and theological trouble in
the passage. The trouble here, let it be noted, is not that Jesus needs a
break. Christians who, like me, want to live within the mainstream of the
historic Christian faith accept that Jesus is truly human, "very man of
very man" as the Nicene Creed declares. He knows our weaknesses
because he has experienced them. It seems to me perfectly natural that
Jesus should be worn down by the demands of the crowd and the hostility of the authorities. Of course he needs a break. Or to put it in more
academically respectable language: The desire for privacy in this pericope is anticipated in the literary structure of the Gospel.

What has always troubled me, rather, is what comes next. Even before
paparazzi and the invention of tabloids, it was hard to keep a secret about
a celebrity. A woman finds out that Jesus is in the house and asks him to
drive a demon from her daughter. Not only is this intruder a woman, but
also she is a foreigner, not a resident of that country. It is one more
request, and it's too much. Let me be clear about this. The problem is not
that I do not understand what comes next. It is that I understand it all too
well. Anybody who has been in parish ministry will understand it, too.
You work and you work and you finally get a chance to sit down for just
a moment's peace and the phone rings. And without fail, it's always the
wrong person on the other end of the line, the one with no social skills
and no sense of your needs as a person. We might remember, moreover,
that the people in our churches understand this feeling perfectly well,
too. In some cases, the "wrong" person on the other end of their line
might even be the minister or priest. It is not, therefore, the case that the
need for rest is troubling. As the letter to the Hebrews says, "For we do
not have a high priest who is unable to sympathize with our weaknesses,
but we have one who in every respect has been tested as we are" (Heb.
4:15). I have argued elsewhere that it is possible to establish in preaching
an analogy between something or someone in the text and something in
our world.[3] In this case, the analogy is far too easy. As the story describes

him, Jesus is worn out and exhausted, as we often are. And, as often happens with us, in that vulnerable state, he is interrupted.

When this happens, Jesus, tired and stressed as he is, says, "It is not fair to take the children's food and throw it to the dogs." By the standards of early third-millennium Western society, this is a terrible thing to say, even to an intruder. In fact, it was probably even more terrible and insulting in first-century Eastern Mediterranean society. Those seeking to minimize the offense note that the word could be translated as "puppies," cute and adorable creatures. But dogs of any age were not "man's best friend," or woman's either, in that society. They were "curs," a symbol for all that was low and despised. When I've been tired and stressed, I've far too often said things I've been ashamed of later. Here we have drawn near the very heart of the problem. I claim Jesus as my Savior and Lord, and I mean no subtle antievangelical irony by that. As I sat there in my study thinking about the text and thinking about Linda's church, I realized that I want my Lord and Savior to be better than I am. In the New Testament as a whole, he is indeed better than I am, infinitely better than I am, almost all the time. Except here. These are hard words, "It is not fair to throw the children's food to the dogs," spoken to the woman's face. To be really honest about it, though I have said many hard things I now wish unsaid, I cannot remember ever saying such stinging words to anyone.

"You have it wrong, Mark," I want to say. "Jesus would never say anything like that!" But there it is in black and white on the page. What's more is that it is in the lectionary, too, and I have to preach from this text next Sunday.

It is sometimes a homiletical advantage to be able to identify some sort of trouble or difficulty in the text. If the trouble is important enough that it is likely to be shared by most of a congregation, it can be a good starting point for an inductive sermon.[4] My difficulty with this text is real, and I imagine that it would be widely shared. If that kind of real and shared problem can be identified, the preacher can then work toward a resolution to the problem in the study. That movement from difficulty toward resolution can subsequently give a structure to the sermon. The preacher leads the listeners toward (hence "inductive" from the Latin, "to lead toward") that resolution in the pulpit. I had thought about this passage before and had heard sermons on it that proposed solutions to the problem. I was not, therefore, starting from scratch. In the sermon, however, one addresses the difficulty as if for the first time.

In an inductive sermon, the preacher might consider raising one or more potential or partial solutions to the initial problem or difficulty raised in the sermon. A partial solution need not be, indeed cannot be, truly satisfying. It may, however, lead to a fuller understanding of the text that eventually will help shape a more satisfying response. At the least, it might clarify our understanding of the problem. One such possibility might be to claim that Jesus was teaching the woman at this moment. Teachers frequently say provocative things they don't truly mean in order to elicit a response from their students. At one point in John's Gospel, Jesus does just that. As the crowd of five thousand streams toward Jesus and the disciples, Jesus says to Philip, one of his followers, "Where are we to buy bread for these people to eat?" (John 6:5). The Gospel of John emphasizes Jesus' godlike knowledge of all things, so the question is immediately interpreted, "He said this to test him for he himself knew what he was going to do." Jesus wanted a response from Philip. Perhaps in our text also, one might argue, he simply wanted a response from the woman. It is impossible to disprove such an interpretation, but it must be acknowledged that there seems to be no hint of any such plan in the words of the text itself. The only reason I would come to such a reading is that I want to find John's calm and all-knowing Jesus in this text from Mark. If I am honest, however, I must confess that such a reading comes from my own desires, not from the text. The most natural interpretation of the story is that Jesus said these words because he meant them.

A more promising approach might be to claim that Jesus' response is shaped by Jesus' inherited culture. The fundamental attitude that led to these words was part of Jesus' time and culture. That is undeniably true. There is an ancient prayer that I normally prefer not to quote. Some listeners might think it tends to put Judaism in a bad light, and we Christians have done quite enough of that over the centuries. It is, however, relevant to the issue at hand.

> Blessed art thou, O Lord our God, who hast not made me a heathen.
> Blessed art thou, O Lord our God, who hast not made me a
> bondman.
> Blessed art thou, O Lord our God, who hast not made me a woman.[5]

(By the way, the prayer book allows the women to say, "Blessed art thou, O Lord our God, who hast made me according to thy will." That may not help much.)

It is not known how old that particular formulation actually is. It could quite possibly, however, have come from a culture very much like the one into which Jesus was born. The gospel came, as it always comes, into a particular culture, a time, a place, and a set of values. What happens in our story should be judged, it could be argued, not just by our standards, but by theirs. It is unfair to beat a first-century text with a twenty-first-century stick.

She was a woman and a Gentile; perhaps she was also a slave. Perhaps in that patriarchal and ethnocentric society, Jesus' behavior is more understandable. All this may even be largely true, but it is hardly satisfying. Let me put it very personally. I want Jesus not only to be better than me, but also I want him to be better than his culture. The Lord and Savior ought to transcend his culture.

When I lift my eyes from this story and consider the Gospel portrait of Jesus as a whole, I see that Jesus does that very thing. He cares about women and he helps foreigners. How did that happen? According to the Gospel of Mark, a feisty, tough, determined woman wouldn't take no—even a rude and dismissive no—for an answer. She cared enough for her child that she stood up even to this foreign rabbi.

"Even the dogs under the table eat the children's crumbs." Jesus recognized something in her answer that was right.

"For saying that, you may go—the demon has left your daughter." And so, according to the story it was: "So she went home, found the child lying on the bed, and the demon gone."

But for a moment let us turn our attention from what happened to the girl or her mother. Let us consider what happened to Jesus. It looks as if he learned something from this encounter. Some of us have only a Gospel of John Christology. Our Jesus knows all things and perceives all things rightly. I for one would never want to dispense with the Christology of the Fourth Gospel. If this picture of Jesus is not balanced by the Jesus of the Synoptic Gospels, however, there can be a problem. Contrary to the historic Christian faith, our Jesus would be not truly human, but superhuman, not "very man of very man," but "superman." Superman, let it be remembered, is either a creation of Friedrich Nietzsche or a comic book figure, depending on our reading habits. In this story, the very human Jesus of the Gospel of Mark learned something new. Perhaps to this point Jesus, like the Pharisees themselves, had been living within the "traditions of the elders." Perhaps now he was recognizing that in yet another way these traditions were inadequate and something less than the "commandment of God."

There is certainly good evidence in the Gospel of Mark that Jesus did learn well from the encounter. Consider the next pericope, the one linked with our text by the Revised Common Lectionary. In it, we are told that Jesus "returned from the region of Tyre, and went by way of Sidon towards the Sea of Galilee, in the region of the Decapolis" (Mark 7:31). Mark takes trouble to let us know that Jesus is staying in Gentile territory. (Matthew, by contrast, is not as precise.) In that territory, Jesus meets a deaf man, by implication a Gentile, and goes to unusual trouble to heal him. The description of the procedure of the healing is one of the most detailed in all the Gospels (Mark 7:33-34). The contrast with our passage is striking indeed.

This is not an unusual interpretation of the text.[6] But I cannot say that it was easy for me to absorb as I studied the text. It may also be difficult for you, and very likely it would be difficult for some of your listeners. I was certain that it would distress some members of a Presbyterian church in rural Ontario. Does this kind of growth suggest that, before this moment, Jesus was at least in this respect incomplete, and was that incompleteness less than divine or even sinful? I was helped, however, by a childhood memory. When I was a child, memory work was still in fashion, and I was made to memorize Bible verses even in public school. I remember being made to memorize Luke 2:52 in the King James Version of the Bible: "And Jesus increased in wisdom and stature, and in favor with God and man." No one has any trouble, to the best of my knowledge, with the notion that Jesus increased in stature. Nobody thinks Mary laid a full-grown Jesus in the manger. On a more theological level, no one would ever suggest that physical growth implies a sinful incompleteness. Why should I have difficulty with the complementary notion that Jesus increased in wisdom? If all that is true, my acute discomfort with this text may have been misplaced. We have a vivid picture in this text of Jesus increasing in wisdom.

So let me go back to orthodox Christian theology. It is a central tenet of our faith that in Jesus we see what it means to be fully human. Perhaps this story teaches us that to be fully human does not mean to be immune to stress. It does not mean being complete every moment of our lives. Being fully human means being ready to grow. It means being willing to learn from even from the most unlikely and surprising people. Judging by this story, it may mean being willing to learn from people our culture or our religion may have taught us to look down on. To live like Jesus is to be ready to grow.

I was pretty sure I could preach that in Linda's church. The sermon might sound politically correct to some listeners, but in my estimation it was just plain correct. I was not ready to end either my work or the sermon at this point, however. On a homiletical level, it genuinely is preferable to end a sermon on a celebratory occasion, such as an anniversary, on a positive note. Besides, I was writing a book on preaching grace, and not much grace had yet made it into this sermon. There was also, however, a niggling question that was purely exegetical. Ending our study here ignores what Mark's Jesus says is the key thing. It is not just that the woman was quick witted, feisty, and stood up to Jesus, nor even that Jesus learned from her. According to Jesus, there is something very right, something that changes the whole situation in *what the woman has said*. What is there about this "dogs under the table" business that is so profoundly right?

There the matter rested for several days without any apparent progress. Then one evening I was complaining to my wife about the difficulties of the sermon while sitting at the dinner table. I have a bad habit of gesticulating while speaking, even when eating. I picked up a slice of bread, laid much too large a slab of butter on it, and waved it about in mid-lament. Off came the butter and landed with a splat on the floor by my feet. Out from under the table like a furry arrow shot our dog, Rupert. He licked up the butter with one swoop of his tongue. If the experts say dogs can't smile, they're very wrong. A dog who lives on dried kibble, and for whom a slab of butter drops unexpectedly from above, can definitely smile. Rupert's smile showed that there is indeed good news in the text. Something wonderful may drop from above when you least expect it. And if you are lying close to the Master's feet, it may fall to you.

The end of the sermon dropped from above. This book belongs to the Great Texts series, and it is about finding grace in biblical texts. Sometimes, however, grace for the preacher is not just uncovered in texts. Sometimes it comes from above as crumbs fall to the dog under the table.[7]

CHAPTER 6

Luke 19:1-10:
To Seek and to Save the Lost

A longtime colleague, Dr. Stanley Walters, used to say in class, "Position is hermeneutic." By that he meant that the meaning of a passage is very much determined by its relationship to the passages around it. At this point we turn to a pair of passages in the Gospel of Luke whose meaning is very much shaped by their position. One, the encounter between Jesus and Zacchaeus, is an obvious choice for a commentary on preaching grace. The other, the parable of the ten coins, seems at first sight a parable of obligation rather than grace. Because of its position, however, we shall be able to find grace in that parable also. We begin, however, with the story of Zacchaeus.

THE LIMITS AND CONTEXT OF THE PASSAGE

The limits of the passage are unmistakable in this case. Luke 19:1-10 is a self-contained story of the encounter between Jesus and Zacchaeus, a rich tax collector. No time need be spent demonstrating this.

The position of this story and of the parable that follows are worthy of extended discussion however. This story appears almost at the climax of the travel narrative that takes up the entire middle section of the Gospel. The travel narrative begins at Luke 9:51 ("When the days drew near for him to be taken up, he set his face to go to Jerusalem") and continues to the end of the parable of the ten coins at Luke 19:27.

There is what appears to be a striking reference to the travel narrative in Luke 9:31. This verse is in the middle of the account of the transfiguration, Luke 9:28-37, a pericope that anticipates many themes that will recur in the Gospel. Luke is an author with highly developed literary skills, so it will be worth our while to trace some of the themes we shall find there. Three disciples, Peter, James, and John are taken aside and grow sleepy (as in Gethsemane). A voice speaks from heaven, not only an echo of the baptism (Luke 3:21-22), but also an anticipation of the angelic message in the empty tomb (Luke 24:5-7) and at the ascension (Acts 1:11). Moses (the law) and Elijah (the prophets) appear and, by their appearance, testify to Jesus' status as the one sent from God. Similarly, the risen Christ will so interpret the scriptures that the law and the prophets bear witness to him on the walk to Emmaus (Luke 24:27) and to the gathered disciples (Luke 24:44). In Luke 9:31, Moses and Elijah "appeared in glory and were speaking of his *departure,* which he was about to accomplish at Jerusalem." The next mention of Jerusalem in the Gospel is the beginning of the travel narrative (Luke 9:51), quoted above. The word *departure* is often interpreted as a reference to the death of Jesus. That is too narrow an explanation, however. It also refers to the resurrection and to the account of the ascension, which concludes the Gospel. Furthermore, there is in all probability a reference to the journey that Jesus and his disciples are about to undertake. The Greek word behind the English *departure* is the journey word par excellence, *exodus.*

The journey, then, is a theological journey, an exodus. One will not expect from a writer as subtle as the third evangelist any mechanical or simplistic correspondence with the account of the first exodus in the Pentateuch.[1] Nevertheless, attentive listeners will strain their ears to catch echoes. There may be broad similarities to the experience of the people of Israel in their desert wanderings. The key similarity lies in the experience of grace; the people of Israel are saved by a God who, out of sheer grace, rescues the people from their misery: "I am the LORD your God, who brought you out of the land of Egypt, out of the house of slavery" (Exod. 20:2, Deut. 5:6). Luke also consistently presents a picture of a people saved by renewed grace. Another key similarity lies in this: In both first and second exodus, there is Torah, instruction of the people in right living. Much of the exodus narrative in the Pentateuch answers the question "What does a life shaped by a covenant relationship with the God who rescued the people from Egypt look like?" Much of the travel narrative of the Gospel of Luke answers the question, "What does a life shaped by grace look like?"

Grace is indeed a key and repeated theme of the travel narrative. We hear of a Samaritan binding up the wounds of a beaten Jew, a woman seeking a coin, and a shepherd seeking a lost sheep, a host welcoming in the outcast to a banquet, and a father rejoicing over the return of a much loved son. These are but a few references that could easily be multiplied among parables, sayings, and miracle stories. Grace is the very rhythm of the steps on the journey to Jerusalem.

Another key and repeated theme is less obvious: the use of possessions, especially money. The following list of references to the use of money does not pretend to be exhaustive.[2] The only purpose of what follows is to show that money is indeed a significant theme in the travel narrative. The seventy are to take no purse on their mission (10:4). The Samaritan pays the innkeeper (10:35). The Pharisees neglect right alms but tithe even for their spices (11:41-42). Sparrows are sold for two pennies, and humans are infinitely more valuable (12:5). A rich fool builds barns (12:13-21). The disciples are to sell their possessions, give alms, and secure for themselves treasure in heaven (12:32-35). Don't invite your rich neighbors to dinner, the ones who can pay you back, but rather invite the poor. A man gave a great dinner, but the invited guests, some preoccupied with the use of their resources, refused to come. Instead, the poor, the lame, and the blind were ushered in (14:12-24). The one who builds a tower counts the cost (14:28-29). No one can become a disciple without selling his or her possessions (14:33). A woman seeks a lost coin (15:8-10). A younger son demands his share of the property (15:11-32). A dishonest manager is fired for wasting money (16:1-8 [9-13]). The Pharisees love money (16:14). There was a rich man and, outside his gate, a beggar named Lazarus (16:19-31). A Pharisee who gives a tenth of his income goes to the temple to pray. Next to him is a tax collector (18:9-14). (Clearly, that parable ought to be kept in mind when we read our text.) A rich man asks Jesus what he must do to inherit eternal life: "Sell all that you own." He was sad for he was very rich. "How hard it is for those who have wealth to enter the kingdom," like a camel through the eye of a needle (18:18-30). Here we are getting very near the immediate context of our passages, so the exercise may be laid aside for the moment. What can be confidently said is that Luke's Jesus is interested in what people do with their money.[3]

The final complex within the travel narrative begins with the third and final prediction of the passion[4] and carries through the story of the triumphal entry into Jerusalem. It will be useful to consider this complex as a whole before dealing with our texts. As at the beginning of the travel narrative, we are reminded of the goal of the journey: "See, we are going up to Jerusalem" (18:31). The events that are to come—betrayal, suffering, death, and resurrection—are then set out with astonishing specificity. The Son of Man, we are told, will certainly suffer rejection. This clearly anticipates the final section of the Gospel, the passion narrative. It also alerts the readers that everything that follows must be interpreted in light of the cross and resurrection. But the disciples do not understand what they have been told (18:34, cf. 19:11).

The journey then resumes. As they draw near to Jericho, they encounter a blind beggar, a poor man. He shouts out, "Jesus, Son of David, have mercy on me." Note that the beggar addresses Jesus with a royal title. He is hailing Jesus as a kingly figure. But the recognition of Jesus' royal status provokes a reaction. Those in the front try to silence Bartimaeus (cf. the Pharisees in 19:39-40), but he repeats his cry. The repetition ought to make even the slowest reader grasp the significance of his words. Jesus, by heeding the appeal, implicitly accepts the royal designation.

It also ought to be noted that the appeal "have mercy on me!" is an appeal for nothing less than grace. And Jesus extends to Bartimaeus that grace; he grants him his sight. This may be a contrast to the disciples who cannot "see" in the spiritual sense. Grace rightly received then leads to a response (cf. the story of the ten lepers in 17:11-19). Bartimaeus follows Jesus; in effect, he becomes a disciple. As a disciple, Bartimaeus offers praise to God, and that praise is catching. The story is one of grace and response, in this case discipleship and praise. This brings us to the story of Zacchaeus.

VERSES 1-4, THE VIEW FROM A TREE

On his "exodus" to Jerusalem, Jesus passes through Jericho. As even a glance at a map of Palestine will show, this is indeed an odd route for a company on the way from Galilee to Jerusalem.[5] It is both out of the way and very much downhill. (Jericho is near the Dead Sea, the lowest place on the planet.) Walkers in the mountains do not willingly lose height. The walk back uphill, as from Jericho to Jerusalem, is always tiring. But it may be that the route is more theological than geographical. Perhaps this is an echo of the culmination of the Old Testament exodus in which the people enter the promised land at Jericho. The attentive reader might even remember that the only named inhabitant of Jericho in that ancient story was a prostitute named Rahab, in other words, a sinner.

Whether or not that detail was in the author's mind, we are introduced at this point by name to an inhabitant of Jericho. This is, of course, Zacchaeus, who "was a chief tax collector and was rich." Both descriptions are interesting. The Romans governed their vast empire with the aid of a surprisingly small bureaucracy. The administration of the empire depended in large part upon the assistance of collaborators from among the governed peoples. In particular, taxes were collected by locals who bid for the right to do so. They collected taxes with only the most minimal supervision. To collect tolls and taxes was therefore to have a magnificent opportunity for corruption. The advice of John the Baptist to tax collectors is, "Collect no more than the amount prescribed for you" (Luke 3:13). Zacchaeus was, according to the story, a "chief" tax collector. Jericho, by virtue of its location on ancient trade routes, and because of upwelling springs in the area, was a wealthy city. Zacchaeus was therefore, as the text tells us, rich. It is reasonable to suppose both from what we know of the history of the period and from the reaction of the crowd in this story (v. 7) that a wealthy tax collector would be hated. The crowd will eventually tell us the third important piece of information about Zacchaeus. He is a chief tax collector, rich, and also a sinner.

The reader of Luke's Gospel knows, however, that Jesus does not hate the tax collectors. He had called a tax collector as a disciple and ate with him and his fellows (Luke 5:27-32). He told a parable in which a repentant tax collector goes home justified (Luke 18:9-14). Indeed, his welcoming attitude to these people is a chief complaint against Jesus (Luke 5:30, 7:34, 15:1-3). To be truthful, that the reader of, and the listener to, contemporary sermons knows that Jesus accepts tax collectors is potentially a homiletical problem. It might rob the story of surprise and, in doing so, prevent us from seeing grace in it.

Although tax collectors are more or less sympathetic figures in the Third Gospel, it is not so with the rich. Very near the beginning of the Gospel, we are told that the rich are sent away empty (Luke 1:53). Luke's version of the Beatitudes is terribly blunt about their fate: "But woe to you who are rich" (Luke 6:24). By contrast, the poor are "blessed." A rich man can be a "fool" in a parable (Luke 12:13-21). A rich man in another parable can ignore the poor beggar at his gate and be consigned to Hades (Luke 17:19-30). Above all, a rich man with every claim to human righteousness can so love his wealth that he cannot hear Jesus' command to give it away to the poor (Luke 18:18-30). (That passage ought to be kept firmly in mind as we read the story of Zacchaeus.) The reader may be predisposed to accept that Jesus will forgive and welcome a tax collector. There should be no such favorable disposition with respect to a rich man. The reader knows already: "Indeed, it is easier for a camel to go through the eye of a needle than for someone who is rich to enter the kingdom of God" (Luke 18:25).

Luke is a marvelous storyteller, intertwining his material with previous passages. In both our story and the story of blind Bartimaeus that precedes it, the bystanders play a significant role. In the first place, in both pericopes, there are people between Jesus and the one in need. In the Bartimaeus story, there is a reference to "those who are in the front." In the second, the "vertically challenged" Zacchaeus ("a wee little man was he," according to the children's song) must climb a sycamore tree to see Jesus over the bystanders.

At this point in the story, some commentators and many preachers indulge in overly psychological interpretations of the text. Zacchaeus is short, we are told. This becomes a metaphor in some sermons for inadequacy and human need. This is an overly symbolic interpretation of the text. There are some indications in passages such as the story of King Saul that the Hebrews admired the tall, but there is no indication that they scorned those of lesser stature. The word *short* has no strong negative connotations. It is better to take the description at face value; Zacchaeus cannot see Jesus over the crowd. (Perhaps one might suppose that they were unwilling to make way for the sinner, but that, too, goes beyond the text.) The one thing that the text tells us of the state of Zacchaeus's mind and spirit is that "he was trying to see Jesus." The Greek word behind the English "trying to" is very interesting, however. It is, in fact, the verb that is often rendered by some form of "to seek." Zacchaeus is a "seeker." As a result, he takes extraordinary and, in that culture, undignified steps, very quickly, by running ahead and climbing a tree. He is very eager indeed to see Jesus.

Preachers often expand on this point, speculating, perhaps with good reason, that Zacchaeus is dissatisfied with his life of wealth and isolation. He has heard, we say, that this rabbi will welcome even sinners such as tax collectors. This may well be true, but the text does not tell us any of this. Not only would it be faithful to the text not to identify too precisely Zacchaeus's motives in seeking Jesus, but also it would be, as we shall see, homiletically advantageous as well. The interpreter might more safely concentrate, however, not on what went on in the mind of Zacchaeus, but on what goes on now in the mind of the reader. The reader of Luke knows ever more clearly the mind and character of Jesus and, by this point, should understand well that he will welcome even tax collectors. The reader is prepared by Luke, the master storyteller, for an instance of that love for sinners that we have learned to call "grace."

VERSES 5-10, THE ENCOUNTER

To this point, Zacchaeus has been the chief actor in the story. He is the one who "was seeking to see Jesus" (my translation of verse 3). Now Jesus takes on that role. In the first place, he invites himself to dinner. The "hospitality of grace"[6] does not stand upon etiquette. There is a necessity about the coming of Jesus to the house of the sinner: "Hurry and come down; for I must come to your house today." The words are rich with theological meaning. The encounter is not a chance event resulting from, for all we know, a momentary whim of Zacchaeus. It is a necessity for Zacchaeus and for Jesus alike. It is part of the plan of the one who creates all necessities.

"Today" is the moment of salvation. The Greek behind this word is the *day* of the angel's announcement, "To you is born *this day* . . . a savior" (Luke 2:11, emphasis mine). It is the word Jesus speaks in the synagogue at Nazareth, "*Today* this scripture has been fulfilled in your hearing" (Luke 4:21, emphasis mine). That day has now arrived for Zacchaeus. He must hurry down and receive it, and he does so. "So he hurried down and was happy to welcome him." *Happy* may be too light a translation. He welcomes Jesus, "rejoicing." Such joy is the appropriate response to grace.

The reader will not be surprised by all this, but the crowd is. As in the story of Bartimaeus, there is a problem caused by the bystanders. In the former story, those in front try to silence the beggar. In our story, they grumble and complain. It remains, perhaps, too often true that those around Jesus try to impede the progress of grace. More important, their words, like the words of Jesus, are rich with meaning.

It is sometimes the case in the Gospels that an unsympathetic character is made unwittingly to speak the truth. The best-known example of this can be found in the Gospel of John in 18:14, in which the high priest Caiaphas is the one who knows that "it [is] expedient that one man should die for the people" (KJV). Luke, too, uses the technique of putting key words in the mouth of unsympathetic characters. See, for example, the words of Simon the Pharisee at Luke 7:39, the words of the evil spirit through the slave girl at Acts 16:17, or the words of the hostile crowd concerning the apostles in Acts 17:6-7. So it is here also. The crowd's grumbling complaint speaks the absolute and beautiful truth: "He has gone to be the guest of one who is a sinner." This is what Jesus characteristically does; he joins those who are sinners. Note the direction of the action: Jesus does not invite the sinner to the house of God. (This is so often the direction of our evangelism.) Rather, he must go to the house of the sinner.

Note that the grumblers are correct in their analysis of the spiritual state of Zacchaeus. Like Simon the Pharisee, these people have "judged rightly" (Luke 7:43). The rest of the story makes little sense unless Jesus, like the bystanders, recognizes Zacchaeus as a sinner. Contemporary Christians are often extremely uncomfortable with the word *sinner*. The Gospel is not; it tells us that Zacchaeus is a sinner. The difference between Jesus and the bystanders is not in the diagnosis of Zacchaeus's condition. All agree he is a sinner. The difference lies in the treatment. They scorn; Jesus loves. Or to put it slightly differently, the difference is grace.

In dramatic homiletical presentations of the story, Jesus then has dinner with Zacchaeus. This table fellowship is understood as the gracious acceptance that provokes the response in Zacchaeus. The text does not specify, however, that the meal takes place at this point. Rather, what comes next is most naturally read as an immediate response to the complaint of the bystanders. Perhaps even the summons to table fellowship is in itself sufficient for salvation.

One might debate the timing of the meal; what is beyond debate is that this pericope is a classic story of grace. Like that of blind Bartimaeus, this is a story of grace that reaches out to help one who cannot help himself. Moreover, as in that story, there is a response to grace. As is fitting for and from a rich "sinner" whose sins may well have been financial, the response to grace involves money: "Look, half of my possessions, Lord, I will give to the poor; and if I have defrauded anyone of anything, I will pay back four times as much." Zacchaeus makes this fascinating statement, it should be noted, as a defense not to the crowd, but to Jesus. He must demonstrate his sincerity first to Jesus. As in the first text studied in this book, 2 Corinthians 8, there is no more convincing evidence of sincerity than cash money. Zacchaeus puts his money where his mouth is, or, to put it in more biblical terms, where his heart is.

In stark contrast to the last rich man in the Gospel of Luke, Zacchaeus gives willingly. He does not content himself merely with what the law requires. Unlike the rich young ruler, he does not concern himself with what he must "do to inherit eternal life." Eternal life has invited itself to his house for lunch, and in gratitude (a word that is derived etymologically from grace), he offers freely what he has. As the commentators note, the sums are beyond the requirements of the law, with respect to restitution. Numbers 5:6-7 stipulates that, in cases of wrongdoing, full restitution must be paid, plus one-fifth or 20 percent. Even if "four times as much" actually means eighty percent as opposed to four hundred percent, this is a huge sum of money. One might ask, "How can Zacchaeus possibly afford this?" But "How much?" is never a question posed by grace. Grace is mercy pressed down and running over. It overflows, as in Zacchaeus, with generosity. Grace evokes grace; there is a "multiplication factor" involved.

Jesus, as chief actor in the drama, has the last word: "Today salvation has come to this house." "Today" has indeed become the moment of salvation. The word *salvation* here denotes the restoration of right relationships. Zacchaeus is now in a right relationship with Jesus. He is also in right relationship with his possessions. He can give his possessions away to meet human need and to achieve the reconciliation with others in the community, which is the aim of the commandment. That last set of relationships cannot be entirely achieved by Zacchaeus or even by Jesus. The community must welcome the sinner also, always a problem in the Gospel of Luke (cf. Luke 15:1-3). At this point, it is clear that Jesus is speaking not to Zacchaeus, but to the bystanders, for he refers to Zacchaeus in the third person, "because he too is a [child] of Abraham." The name *Abraham* is rich with meaning. In the first place, it reminds the bystanders of the identity that they share with Zacchaeus. They are all children of Abraham. Indeed, in the Gospel of Luke, it is even possible to be overly proud of one's identity as a child of Abraham. God can even make children of Abraham from stones (Luke 3:8) or, for that matter, from chief tax collectors. The word also reminds the reader of the covenant promises of God (cf. Luke 1:54-55 and 72-73). It is God's intention to create not only renewed individuals, but also a renewed people.

In the end, Jesus says, "The Son of Man has come to seek and to save the lost." What could be a more succinct statement of the meaning of grace? At the beginning of the story, it appears that Zacchaeus is the seeker. All our attention is focused on him. In the very deepest sense, however, the one great seeker is Jesus.

PREACHING GRACE FROM LUKE 19:1-10

The key to preaching this passage might be to allow our listeners to draw analogies between themselves and figures in the text. It would be possible to suggest an analogy between ourselves and the righteous bystanders who get in the way of grace. That is hardly the most inviting option for preaching grace from this passage, however. It would be more gracious to preach to those who can see themselves up the tree with Zacchaeus.

I wrote earlier that it is homiletically advantageous as well as faithful to the text not to be overly precise about the motives that made Zacchaeus climb a sycamore tree. We are not told and do not know his motives. This very lack of specificity, however, makes his situation more nearly analogous to our own. It is here, perhaps, that we might recognize ourselves and the people to whom we preach. If we are not overly precise, that is to say, if we do not identify Zacchaeus's need too specifically with his situation as a tax collector for a foreign power, our listeners will more easily link themselves to him. (In some circles in society, the idea of going to a church to find someone who might meet our needs would be considered as strange and ridiculous as climbing a sycamore tree.) In truth, we do not know the exact nature of Zacchaeus's need, whether it was loneliness, isolation, the scorn of others, or the misery of possessing everything he thought he had wanted but not the one thing he needed. For that matter, it is possible that a person such as Zacchaeus might not even know his own motives. We only know that he was lost and needed to be found. Can we not say very similar things about ourselves? If so, the third pew from the back on the left-hand side in our church might actually become a sycamore tree. If that pew does become a sycamore tree, Jesus will find the people sitting there.

Those of us who preach in wealthy or relatively wealthy North American churches might also want to note that this is a story of grace that reaches a rich man. The Gospel of Luke is not simpleminded in its preference for the poor. Luke's Jesus will seek out the rich as well as the poor. The only qualification for his care is that the person be lost. Both rich and poor may receive grace. By that grace, it is even possible for a camel to pass through the eye of a needle. There are, however, very likely financial consequences to being swept up by grace. Whatever else true grace may be, it isn't cheap. Perhaps every honest sermon on grace ought to come with a label, "Warning: Grace may be dangerous to your financial health."

CHAPTER 7

Luke 19:11-27: Grace Multiplying

Preaching grace is more than selecting passages in which the word itself appears or in which the mercy and love of God are plainly the subject of the text. It is also a matter of looking for grace in texts that have usually been preached primarily as obligation. Make no mistake; there are indeed many texts in the Bible that declare to us our duty as followers of Jesus Christ. The faithful preacher may not avoid those texts or soft-pedal the demand that is found in them. Demand always rests upon grace, however. It is likely to be there in the context of the demand, and, if we look closely enough, it may also be found in the text that declares the demand. The link between grace and demand lies in this: What God demands is a life shaped by grace.

To illustrate these points, let us consider a parable of Jesus that follows immediately upon the story of Zacchaeus. Though the parable clearly lays an obligation upon us, we shall also find in it a word of grace. This is, however, at first sight a "law" parable that might be preached moralistically. It is likely, however, that we shall find grace aplenty in it, especially if we read it in light of its position in the Gospel.

The parables of Jesus are sometimes treated as if they are primarily to be valued as clues to the teaching or spiritual consciousness of a first-century religious figure whose life may be reconstructed from the careful sifting of materials in the "five Gospels."[1] They may also be studied to determine developments in the very early days of the Christian tradition. In short, they are sometimes examined in much the same way that an archaeologist excavates an ancient mound. The scholar attempts to dig beneath the surface of the mound to uncover the earliest possible layer of material. The surface itself is of little interest to the archaeologist. There are two difficulties with this approach. In the first place, the results of the excavation are very likely to be speculative. Second, the "surface" of the mound that is ignored is the scripture itself, as we know it. That scripture was carefully arranged and composed so that, in it, communities and persons of faith might find truth and meaning. For the purposes of preaching, parables are often most fruitfully interpreted in their canonical narrative contexts. [2]

Consider this parable, which I once composed:

> There was a householder who lived by a lake. It was the custom of the householders by the lakes in that country to set out feeders for the hummingbirds. They filled the feeders with red sugared water. And the hummingbirds were drawn to the feeders by the bright color and drank and were fed. And all who saw them were delighted by the beauty and the grace of the birds who came to feed. The householder prepared red water for the feeder but into it placed not sugar, but aspartame. The hummingbirds came and came again, for they were drawn by the color and by the sweetness of the water, and the householder was glad. But the hummingbirds died of starvation.

There would be several ways to interpret this little parable. One might, for example, attempt to use the parable to draw a picture of its author. (He was probably a person who lived by a lake and was a birder. One inference would be true and the other false. He could not have composed the parable before the invention of aspartame in the late twentieth century—completely true but of little theological use.) It would be more fruitful, however, to note that the parable stands within a book about biblical interpretation and preaching, specifically about preaching grace. It would also be reasonable to consider its immediate context, a discussion of the most nourishing ways of interpreting parables for preaching. Similarly, the infinitely more significant parable of the coins ought to be considered in its literary context also.

THE CONTEXT OF THE PASSAGE

Much of this material has already been considered at length in the previous chapter. We ought to remember, however, that in this part of the Gospel of Luke we find a repeated emphasis on grace and money. From the story of Zacchaeus, we learn that a right response to grace may lie in the use of money. There are other significant themes also in the preceding material. We have heard of rejection and death for the Son of Man and misunderstanding by the disciples. We have heard Jesus hailed with a royal title. We have witnessed two scenes of grace and two responses to that grace. One of those responses involves money and a "multiplication factor."

Some of these themes will not just recur, but resound, like a shouted hosanna through the pericopes that follow. In the story of the triumphal entry, the pericope that immediately follows our parable, Luke, unlike Matthew, does not cite Zechariah 9:9 with its explicit royal language. This is in line with Luke's more subtle and indirect use of the Old Testament. Luke uses allusions in which Matthew gives quotations. But even if the reader were to miss the significance of the figure arriving on a donkey, or the equally pressing allusions to Psalm 118, it is impossible to miss the words of the crowd of disciples, "Blessed is the *king* who comes in the name of the Lord!" (Luke 19:38, emphasis mine). Once again, Jesus is hailed as king. Like Bartimaeus, the disciples shout out in a loud voice, and, like him, they praise God. But, as is the case so often in the Gospel, there is also opposition. The Pharisees urge Jesus to silence his disciples, just as the bystanders tried to silence Bartimaeus. Those who hail Jesus as king will not be silenced, however. If they were to be silent, even the stones would cry out.

The story of the triumphal entry must be read in light of the prediction of the passion that begins this complex in the Gospel and also in light of the story of the passion itself that follows. The disciples are shouting out the right words and cannot be silenced, but in light of what follows, it must be asked whether they truly understand what they have said. Their welcome is a misunderstanding and even, possibly, a rejection. At this point, a tragic note enters or, rather, as we shall see, recurs in the narrative. Jesus weeps over Jerusalem, for the city does not know the things that make for peace and surely will suffer for that failure.

We are now almost prepared to read the parable of the ten pounds in its Lukan context.[3] Before proceeding further, however, a methodological note is in order. The interpreter reading a parable within the context of the Gospel narrative will see many points of contact with the surrounding material and will almost certainly be led to abandon the "one-point" tradition of parable interpretation. A reading that recognizes hints of meaning at multiple locations in the parable, veiled and ambiguous though those hints may be, is a likely result. Such a reading is in line with some recent scholarly work and is homiletically more fruitful than the older approach.

VERSE 11, THE OCCASION OF THE PARABLE

The purpose within the Gospel of the parable of the pounds is clearly given. "As they were listening to this, he went on to tell a parable, because he was near Jerusalem [the goal of the entire travel narrative], and because they supposed that the kingdom of God was to appear immediately." Apparently the listeners, once again, misunderstand the significance of what they have seen and heard. The significance of this failure should not be underestimated. Failure to understand is a form of rejection. It anticipates the greater rejection that will follow in the passion narrative. In a profound way, however, "they" also get it right. The problem is not that they supposed that the kingdom of God was to appear, but that they supposed it was to happen immediately. They are quite correct to look at Jesus and see something that raises hope that the kingdom has drawn near. What is that "something"? In light of the immediate context, the stories of Bartimaeus and Zacchaeus, we may answer with confidence. They have seen grace, and that, quite rightly, has given them hope for the kingdom.

Who are "they" who misunderstand? Probably they are the disciples who have accompanied Jesus on the journey, but perhaps the identification is left a little uncertain so Luke's readers may identify themselves with the "they" also. This matter of identification is a key one for the interpretation of the parable. The parable is not "aimed at" Jews who, in the early decades of the century, may have rejected Jesus of Nazareth. It is written for "Theophilus" and beyond him for a congregation of Christians, possibly a mixture of Jews and Gentiles, perhaps mostly Gentile, in the last decades of the century. It is most probably they who wonder whether the kingdom will be established in the near future. It is they who need instruction on what to do in the meantime.

Verses 12-14, the Nobleman's Departure

Luke, unlike Matthew, specifies the social status of the chief figure in the parable.[4] The protagonist is a nobleman who is going on a journey to seek royal status. Any reader familiar with the history of Palestine would recognize him immediately as Archelaus, son of Herod the Great:

> At that time (4 B.C.) Archelaus journeyed to Rome to get his kingship over Judaea confirmed; at the same time a Jewish embassy of fifty persons also went to Rome in order to resist his appointment. The sanguinary revenge inflicted upon the people by Archelaus after his return had never been forgotten.[5]

The parallel to verses 12 and 14 of our parable is clear. This historical link ought not to blind us to a more immediate literary link, however. The parable depicts the journey of a royal personage in which the claim to royal power is at issue. That might also serve as a summary of this part of Luke's travel narrative. We are in the midst of a narrative in which Jesus accepts royal titles from Bartimaeus and the disciples, but in which others reject his royal status. Surely we ought to be thinking not of Archelaus only, but of Jesus himself also.[6] In any case, given the surrounding material, it is no surprise that the theme of kingship arises in the parable.

The surrounding material also suggests that there will be grace in the parable. It is there, of course, in the gift of the pounds or minas.[7] Unlike Matthew's version of the parable, the gifts are "a very small thing," as the master says in verse 16, but this point may be left aside for the moment. The nobleman gives gifts to ten servants, but only three servants figure in the development of the story. This, if discussed at all in the scholarly literature, is generally treated as a problem, perhaps as a sign of the awkwardness of the conflation of two original parables,[8] as a survival from an earlier form of the parable, or as a result of clumsy composition by Luke. But as a general rule, Luke is neither awkward in his use of sources nor infelicitous in his own writing. A preaching possibility is to see this as an extension of grace. Matthew may do something similar by increasing the amount of the gifts. In both cases, there is generosity beyond what is necessary or expected. Strictly speaking, gifts need to be given only to two servants to make the story work, but grace is not limited by necessity, literary or otherwise. It reaches those it does not need to reach. One can imagine a homiletical turn here. This may have no root in anything other than the contemporary preacher's imagination, but perhaps not; the evangelists were more like preachers than New Testament scholars. The preacher might ask in an echo of a question Jesus has already asked in the travel narrative in Luke 17:17: "Where are the other seven servants?" The excess of servants is an excess of grace; it also gives the preacher and perhaps Luke the opportunity to "contemporize" the parable. There are still seven servants! It may be with these seven that the listener can identify.

VERSES 15-27, THE RETURN OF THE KING

We may also expect to see a response to grace that will involve the use of money. This is, of course, a necessity of the parable's plot, but it will hardly surprise the reader who has noted the persistence of this theme through the travel narrative. The first servant summoned has turned the one pound into ten. Note the "multiplication factor" as in the Zacchaeus story. The multiplication factor is not merely fourfold; it is tenfold, an amazingly large return.[9] This could lead to despair in an alert listener. "If I cannot produce at these tremendous rates of return, will I, when summoned to account, be rebuked?" But there is grace here, too. People simply do not earn a tenfold return on their investments in normal life. The absurdly great multiplication of the investment shows that we are in the economy of grace, not the economy of investment. The increase is the increase of the mustard seed in the garden or of the yeast in three measures of flour (13:18-21). It is a gift of God and not merely a human work.

The absurdity of this first multiplication pales, however, before the absurdity of a second. The master, noting that the servant has been faithful in "a very small thing" rewards the servant with authority over ten cities. That is a multiplication factor as generous and as extreme as the "hundredfold" of the parable of the sower. It is truly absurd to give such a rich reward for the careful management of a very small sum.[10] Perhaps it is as absurd as filling a banquet table with derelicts, or leaving ninety-nine to seek one lost sheep, or welcoming home a young scoundrel who has blown half the family fortune. Or perhaps it's just grace. As a passing literary observation, it may show us why Luke has the master give the servants such a trivial sum.

A second servant is likewise rewarded, but then the story changes. The parable may contain grace, but if so, grace, it seems, also contains within it a threat. A third servant has responded differently. This servant has, as it were, left the money in the sock drawer because he knows the master is a "harsh man" who takes what he has not deposited and reaps where he has not sown. As if to emphasize the harshness, the words of the frightened servant are repeated against him and what he has is taken from him and given to the first servant, yet another increase. This provokes a complaint from another unnamed "they." The complaint implies the action is unfair. Whatever grace may be, it certainly isn't fair. A generalizing theological response is then offered, "I tell you, to all those who have . . . "

There the story might end. But it does not. The harshness of the story has been emphasized already by the repetition of the third servant's words. Now the master orders that the opposition be "liquidated." Surely it is true that this corresponds thematically to the prediction of the destruction of Jerusalem in 19:41-44, but there Jesus weeps over the city. This hard man delights in the destruction. Luke seems to be importing the mores of tin-pot despots ancient and modern into the Gospel. It is easy enough to hear the voice of the historical Archelaus at this point, but can one hear Jesus? The text is very near becoming, as Richard Rohrbaugh has hinted, "a text of terror."[11]

In the end, we are left with an "is and is not" sort of parable. So much of the parable seems to fit the situation of Jesus as depicted in this part of the Gospel of Luke. So many themes recur in our parable. In one key way, moreover, Jesus is indeed like Archelaus, the historical antecedent of the parable. He is rejected by those who might be his subjects. But Jesus is neither the harsh man of the parable nor the Archelaus of history. He is indeed the one who claims a kingship, but it is a different sort of kingship. He is indeed a "Son of David," but one who stops to heal the blind. He is the one who rebukes by his example the harshness of those who would reject the miserable offender, Zacchaeus. And he is the king who weeps over the rebellious city. In the end, the parable just doesn't "sound like Jesus" as we see him in the passages we have considered. It appears that we need an "is and is not" sort of interpretation for the parable.

Such a means of interpretation is at hand in the travel narrative itself; it is found in the classic rabbinic "light and heavy" technique. The form of such an argument is this: "What is true of the light, the earthly, and less important, is even more true of the heavy, the heavenly, and more important." Luke 11:11-13 is clearly a light and heavy argument: "If you who are evil know how to give good gifts to your children, how much more will the heavenly Father give the Holy Spirit to those who ask him!" In that argument, God is and is not like the father. In our parable, Jesus is and is not like Archelaus.[12] It is true that the obvious verbal markers of the light and heavy argument are not present in our parable as they are in 11:11-13, but it is certainly possible to read the parable in a light and heavy fashion.

If an Archelaus figure can give gifts to his servants, how much more will the Son of David do? If using those gifts produces immense multiplication, how much more will the gifts of the Lord multiply? But this parable refuses to let us look only on the bright side of life. We have learned from Frederick Buechner that the gospel is not just comedy or fairy tale. It is also tragedy. And there is tragedy both in the parable and in the world. If rejecting an Archelaus has dreadful consequences, how much more is it true with the king who comes in the name of the Lord?

There may, however, be still a little too much common prudence in this reading, a little too much of the wisdom of this world, even if it is wisdom that we along with Jesus and Luke can learn from the rabbis. We can stretch after a still deeper wisdom. Grace has little to do with prudence, and if we wish to preach grace, we cannot stop with prudence.

PREACHING GRACE FROM LUKE 19:11-27

There is a popular saying that might serve as a summary and a title of a moralistic sermon on this text: "Use it or lose it!" One can imagine that very phrase on the church sign as the title of next Sunday's sermon. In this light, the parable seems wholly pragmatic and, indeed, imbued with the values of our market and investment-driven society.[13] (The Greek word from which *pragmatic* is derived even appears in the parable in verse 13.) There is a grave danger here that Jesus may become little more than a motivational speaker or personal trainer of the spiritual variety. But if this happens, we are preaching what Paul might call the "wisdom of this world" and not the gospel of grace as shown us by Luke's Jesus. We need to preach a meaning beyond the obvious one that correlates so neatly with contemporary secular piety.

Whatever one's estimate of the value of the work of the Jesus Seminar, surely he or she is correct in this; there is a subversive element in the teaching of Jesus the parabler. In this parable, Jesus subverts a world in which the height of spiritual wisdom would be advice to invest regularly in a spiritual IRA. In hearing Jesus, we enter a world of amazing, pressed-down, thousandfold grace in which a master far different from Archelaus takes our pittance of faithfulness and multiplies it in ways that the prudent and cautious will never know.

But paradoxically that grace does not obviate the need for a faithful response. It is possible to reject Jesus as king not only by outright refusal to welcome him, but also by misusing those resources he has given to us. There is a "bottom-line" faithfulness to a life shaped by grace. There are still seven servants left, and they had better consider again just who their master is, what he gives, and what he demands. The parable does lay on us a demand for faithful response with what we have been given. It need not, however, be preached only as demand. In the Gospel context of the parable, there is "grace abounding." Interpreted in the light of that context, the parable itself shows us grace as well, in fact, grace multiplying. Investing the coins of our time and effort in the service of this king returns the investment, if not a thousandfold, at least handsomely.

Grace in the Old Testament

CHAPTER 8

Genesis 4:1-16: The Blood That Cries Out

Ann Weems, in the title poem of her collection *Putting the Amazing Back in Grace*, writes:

I have reached for rainbows.
I have searched for shalom.
I have shared my family faith stories.
I have knelt in Bethlehem.
I have knelt in Jerusalem.
I have cried my laments in the face of God,
and God has continued to leave
stars where I can find them.[1]

In the context of the poem, "family faith stories" appears to mean the stories of Weems's own birth family. It isn't a lovely phrase; it seems more at home in a Christian education class than in a poem, but it is an accurate description of the stories of the Bible as a whole, including the Old Testament. When reading those stories, it is the preacher's task to "reach for rainbows." Long before the rainbow became the logo of gay liberation, it was a symbol of grace. After the terrible deluge of Noah's flood, there is a rainbow.

God says: "I have set my bow in the clouds, and it shall be a sign of the covenant between me and the earth. . . . When the bow is in the clouds, I will see it and remember the everlasting covenant between God and every living creature of all flesh that is on the earth" (Gen. 9:13, 16). (It is interesting to note that in the text, the covenant is a reminder to *God*. The statement, however, is directed as a promise to humanity, so the rainbow functions also as a sign for us.) It is the preacher's task to set forth these signs, to "reach for rainbows," that is, to see the signs of grace in these family faith stories.

We preachers have a tendency to reach not for the rainbow of grace in the Old Testament, but rather for the overseer's lash of obligation. Sometimes, having done so, we then turn around and with appalling *chutzpah* contrast the "law" of the Old Testament with the "gospel" of the New. *Chutzpah,* according to the old joke, is what a man has who murders his father and mother and throws himself on the mercy of the court because he is an orphan. The *chutzpah* of the Christian preacher who demeans the Old Testament is not nearly as humorous a reality.

There is an unfortunate tendency among Christians to think we have a monopoly on grace. Philip Yancey in his valuable book *What's So Amazing About Grace?* tells this story:

> During a British conference on comparative religions, experts from around the world debated what, if any, belief was unique to the Christian faith. They began eliminating possibilities. Incarnation? Other religions had different versions of gods appearing in human form. Resurrection? Again, other religions had accounts of return from death. The debate went on for some time until C. S. Lewis wandered into the room. "What's the rumpus about?" he asked, and heard in reply that his colleagues were discussing Christianity's unique contribution among world religions. Lewis responded, "Oh, that's easy. It's grace."[2]

According to Yancey, the conferees agreed with Lewis. With considerable humility and trepidation, I might beg to differ. Certainly we ought not to hold Lewis responsible for what was evidently a passing remark, reported secondhand. (God guard and protect us all were we required to answer for every passing remark!) But it appears that Lewis confused the characteristic with the unique. Although grace is characteristic of Christianity, or at least we would like it to be, grace is definitely not unique to Christianity. When we turn, for example, to a Jewish prayer book we find a prayer, "Sovereign of all worlds! Not because of our righ-teous acts do we lay our supplications before thee, but because of thine abundant mercies."[3] Nor is this anything new. In the *Shemoneh 'Esreh,* the great prayer of the synagogue from ancient days we read:

> Blessed art Thou, Lord our God . . . who bestowest abundant grace and createst all things and rememberest the promises of grace to the fathers and bringest a Redeemer to their children's children for thy Name's sake out of love." or . . .

> Forgive us our Father, for we have sinned; pardon us, our King, for we have transgressed. For thou forgivest and pardonest.

> To which the people reply:

> "Blessed art thou, Lord, gracious, rich in forgiveness."[4]

It may also be that grace can be found in a religion that does everything in the name of "Allah, the merciful and compassionate." But let us remain with Judaism here. There is grace in the religion of Israel because there is grace in the Scriptures of Israel, which are, of course, also our Old Testament. We simply have to look for it or, more poetically, "reach for rainbows."

In truth, it is not much of a reach. In our English Bible, words such as *grace and gracious,* or particularly "to be gracious" or "to show grace," usually translate the family of words derived from the Hebrew verb *chanan.* It is a sizable and theologically significant word group. Interesting enough, the noun in Hebrew is not always a strictly theological term; it can, as in English, also mean "elegance" or "beauty." That elegance and beauty are a sign of grace in the theological sense of the word is a wonderful thing. But to give but one familiar example of the strictly theological use of the word:

> The LORD bless you and keep you;
> the LORD make his face to shine upon you, and be gracious to you;
> the LORD lift up his countenance upon you, and give you peace.
> (Num. 6:24-26)

The emphasis on grace in the Old Testament is also witnessed by a number of other key Hebrew words that may be rendered as *mercy* or *steadfast love* rather than *grace.* So, for example, the constant celebration in the psalms of *chesed*, steadfast love, is also a celebration of grace. The great Old Testament scholar Walter Zimmerli even translated *chesed* as "covenant grace."[5] One could therefore read, "The covenant grace of God endures forever." That is doubtless an accurate reading, but it doesn't have a poetic ring. Perhaps, however, such verses could be rendered, "The gracious love of God endures forever." There are so many texts in the scriptures of Israel in which grace can be found. In truth, the First Testament is shot through with a rainbow's splendor of grace.

One text in which preachers have traditionally found obligation rather than grace is Genesis 4, the story of Cain and Abel. It is surprising that the text has been excluded from the lectionary. (Is this a result of the tendency of the lectionary to avoid trouble where possible?) It has, however, held a prominent place in the preaching tradition, and at least one phrase from the story has even entered common speech. Perhaps this text may be used to show that it is possible to find grace even in texts in which we do not expect to find it.

THE CONTEXT OF THE PASSAGE

The wider context of this particular story is, of course, the primeval history of the book of Genesis (1–11). Our passage follows the two creation stories of Genesis and the story of disobedience and the Fall. In that latter story, there is human sin, divine punishment, and also a subtle sign of divine favor, the provision of garments for Adam and Eve (Gen. 3:21). We shall also see these motifs in our passage. Moreover, these realities can also be found, although in different forms, in two later tales of the primeval history, Noah's ark and the Tower of Babel. The story of Cain and Abel fits well into its literary context.

This does not greatly help the preacher with a weighty homiletical problem. For many of our listeners, Genesis, in its early chapters particularly, is like the Queen's state coach, a glorious antique, kept in an obscure corner and trotted out only on ceremonial occasions. It is, however, of little use in daily life. Would even the Queen travel to Heathrow Airport by horse and carriage? Would even the most ardent fundamentalist actually live by Genesis? The text may seem utterly foreign to most of our listeners.

Upon reflection, however, we can discern that all around us the dramas of Genesis play themselves out. We are created and come into existence. Ever and again we reject our God. Still we try to be like God and reach out to grasp the fruit that is forbidden to us. We fall, becoming less than we were created to be. Human hand is raised against human hand, and human strikes down human. Our passage, the story of Cain and Abel, is on first inspection a story about violence and murder. As such, it is no more foreign than CNN or our daily newspaper. These texts may be read after the manner of Reinhold Niebuhr who argued that they are "a symbol of an aspect of every historical moment in the life of men."[6] But it may not be precisely the case that these stories are simply parables of what happens constantly. They are, as the text insists, "in the beginning" stories, telling us how we came to be a certain way. They attempt in their own way to say something not just about our nature, but about our history. We are the way we are because we live inescapably within a history, a history of, among other realities, violence. It may be that listeners will now be more ready to believe that we live within a history that seems to lead inescapably to violence.[7] These are stories with echoes, and one doesn't have to listen very hard to hear the echoes of this one. We are "in Adam," says Paul. But to a tragic degree, we are also "in Cain."

No time needs to be spent discussing the limits of this passage. For preaching purposes, verses 1 through 16 can be considered a clear and distinct unit. Though a genealogy is attached to the passage, the boundaries of the narrative itself are unmistakable.

Verses 1-7, a Death Is Foreshadowed

The story is linked to what has gone before by the account of the conception and birth of Cain and Abel. It is clear from the beginning that Cain will be the chief human actor in the story. Eve's words at his birth are quoted. Abel's birth, by contrast, is reported with scarcely an extra word. (The first child always has all the pictures taken.) It is clear, however, that yet another actor is at work in all this: "I have produced a man *with the help of the LORD.*" There is a play on words in the Hebrew that cannot be reproduced in English. The word rendered *produced* sounds like the name *Cain.* Cain, the story tells us, became a farmer, and Abel, in due course, a shepherd. Older commentaries speculate that the tale was born as an aetiology, an explanation of why a particular clan, the Kenites, were wanderers. Very often it is also suggested that the story reflects an early conflict of shepherd and farmer. To paraphrase *Oklahoma*, "Oh the shepherd and the farmer should be friends." The story of Cain and Abel reminds us that they weren't. It is hard to see how either of these observations, even if true, actually help the preacher.

It is far better to consider the tale a "family faith story." In preaching a story, it is often possible simply to retell the story, adding exegetical notes where needed (or merely interesting) until we reach the key point in the narrative. The key point is very likely to be the point at which an analogy to contemporary reality becomes apparent. In this case, however, what at first appears to be the key point may be a misinterpretation of the text. But we are getting ahead of ourselves here, so we return to the beginning.

In the story, two brothers offer sacrifice. Walter Brueggemann, in his magnificent commentary on Genesis, reminds us that repeatedly in Scripture there are two brothers, Cain and Abel, Jacob and Esau, and a parable in which "a certain man had two sons."[8] Was it because of Cain and Abel that the man had two sons in Jesus' story? Relationships with the brother, with the other, are always difficult. In his memoirs, *Blessings in Disguise,* the great actor Alec Guinness, a devout Roman Catholic, tells of making a retreat in a monastery.[9] A monastery is, by definition, a place where all are brothers. At one point, a monk approached him and asked Guinness if he could guess the greatest difficulty of a monk's life. Guinness imagined answers such as no sex or no drink and other such matters. But the monk replied, "Other monks." We know instinctively that relations with the "brother," or for that matter sister, are always a strain.

One brother, Cain, the farmer, offers the fruits of the field, the other, Abel, the shepherd, a blood sacrifice. The Lord prefers the blood. Almost inevitably, the question why will be raised in our minds. On a purely literary level, the answer is easy: It simply has to be that way for the story to work. The Lord has to prefer one to the other for plot purposes. For those for whom that is not a sufficient answer, it might be added that for the Hebrews the life is in the blood (cf. Gen. 9:4). To sacrifice life as an acknowledgment of the Lord and giver of life is an appropriate offering.

Such answers may not be fully adequate, however, for God often appears to be painfully arbitrary, not only in this text, but also in our lives. Some of our listeners notice this and will not be ready to accept easy answers. I preached on this text recently, and after the service, a young man approached me with this question.[10] As we discussed the matter, his beautiful children were tugging at his sleeve. No more conversation with that boring preacher! It became clear to us that the question was not really about the text, but about ourselves. Life seems as arbitrary as the text. Why was he blessed with the happiness of taking those lovely children home for Sunday lunch while others, for whom we had prayed that day, live in such misery? Why am I blessed in too many ways for me to recount while others, as deserving or more deserving, are stricken with sorrow? Neither of us could solve the problem of why God's blessing falls on some and not on others. It is a mystery beyond easy solution, perhaps beyond any human solution at all. Certainly it is a mystery that this text neither addresses nor solves. For this reason, this question, as in church that day, might be better discussed after the sermon rather than in it. For preaching purposes, it might be best to say something such as, "The Lord—who knows why; it does not matter here—prefers the blood" and get on with the story.

Though psychologizing a text is always dangerous, it may safely be noted that there is a certain verisimilitude to the story. Anybody who is either a brother or a sister will recognize what comes next. In an ancient version of "Dad always liked you best!" Cain becomes angry. Though many a contemporary listener will feel that Cain has been treated unfairly in the story, at least he now gets a warning. Sin is crouching like a predator ready to devour, so beware. In our society, sin is often understood in terms of some pavement graffiti near my office, "Sin = sex + drugs." By contrast, our text pictures sin much more dynamically as a predatory beast. The image is a powerful one and accords with the Pauline understanding of sin as a power. It is a useful corrective to the understanding of sin as transgression of external rules that is so common in our society.

To Brueggemann, who reads this passage not so much in the context of Genesis itself as in relation to John Steinbeck's classic novel *East of Eden*, this warning is a key point. It is possible for Cain to master evil. Brueggeman notes that Steinbeck even quotes the Hebrew Bible at the climax of his novel. The protagonist dies with the Hebrew promise to Cain that he can rule over evil on his lips, "Timshel!"—"You will master it!" We cannot discuss here either Steinbeck's apparent optimism about human nature or the debates in the Christian tradition concerning the inevitability of sin. Our spiritual ancestors debated: *"(Non) posse non pec-care"*— "It is (not) possible not to sin." The preacher does not need to resolve that theological debate. Here it is enough to say that in the story, it is certainly possible for Cain not to commit murder. The big theological issues about human capacities aside, it is likewise possible for us not to commit our more heinous crimes. There is no compulsion either in the story or in life that we should become murderers.

It is possible to reach for a rainbow here. "Timshel"—you can master the evil that threatens you and those around you. But possibility becomes obligation so easily; "You must master it," reads the NRSV. The tone of the Lord's statement in these verses is not nearly so much promise as it is warning. In any case, this passage is, let it be repeated, a story, and a story must be read as a whole. Particularly it cannot be read apart from its climax, a climax we will not reach for many more verses. We have not yet reached a rainbow.

Verses 8-12, a Death and Its Consequences

Cain is heedless of the warning, and Abel is heedless of the threat his brother represents. They go together to a field, and there is murder. In an eerie echo of the acceptable sacrifice, lifeblood is poured out. In an equally eerie echo of a question to Adam in the garden, God asks of Cain, "Where is your brother?" And Cain responds, "I do not know. Am I my brother's keeper?"

It is at this point that we preachers butt in. Does Cain not know his responsibility to his brother, to keep him? Why does he reject his plain and obvious duty to keep his brother? His real sin, and the real sin we must avoid, is the failure to carry out the plain and obvious duty of all humans to keep one another. After a few reflections, parallel to the para-ble of the good Samaritan, on the question "Who is my brother?" (answer: everyone, especially those in need), the sermon winds to its inevitable moral and moralizing conclusion: "Dear friends, always remember to act as your brother or sister's keeper."

This is such familiar preaching material that the key phrase even makes its way into an old joke:

Once upon a time, a visitor to the zoo was astonished to see a monkey holding the Bible in one hand and Charles Darwin's *Origin of Species* in the other. The monkey was glancing from one book to the other, lost in thought.

"Monkey, monkey, what are you doing?" asked the visitor.

"It's quite simple," the monkey replied. "I'm trying to decide whether I am my brother's keeper or my keeper's brother."

One wonders how many sermons urging us to be our brother's (or sister's) keeper did it take for that phrase to work its way even into our humor.

Of course, the Bible tells us to love and care for our neighbor. We may not deny even for a moment either that we must care or that we clergy ought to preach the obligation to care. But that plain and clear obligation is not in the focus of the text here. Cain's real sin is not a failure to keep his brother. It is nothing so abstract; it is murder. Moreover, nowhere in Scripture is it said that we ought to be our brother's keeper. To make this pseudo-command the focus of our sermon is to do violence not simply to this story, but to the witness of Scripture as a whole.

Old Testament scholar Paul Riemann wrote a splendid article on this very point. In it he brilliantly mimics the style of various Old Testament writers to carry his point. (The article was written just before the advent of inclusive language.)

> Even if we should give ourselves the whole range of the Old Testament Literature, where is there a text which we could use to rebuke Cain? Is there in Exodus a command, "Thou shalt be thy brother's keeper"? Is there in Deuteronomy some preachment, "Take heed lest you forget to keep your brother, for Yahweh your God kept you in the land of Egypt, in the house of bondage"? Is there perhaps in Proverbs a saying, "The wise man keepeth his brother, but the fool refuseth to be kept"?? Or in the Psalms, "Blessed is the man who keeps his brother"? No, indeed there is not; neither these nor anything like them.[11]

Riemann claims convincingly that the verb *keep* in the Old Testament always implies a relationship of basic inequality in which the keeper is the superior. Note, for example, that in the creation story, Adam is called to "keep" the garden (Gen. 2:15), but not the partner fit for him. There are indeed several instances in the book of Esther in which an official is described as a keeper of the women, or of the harem. These examples, however, prove Riemann's point rather than deny it. One does not "keep" a free and equal partner. These are indeed "kept women" in the terrible old English phrase. In fact, the connotations of the Hebrew verb are in this respect very similar to its English equivalent. Think of the way we use the word *keeper* in English. Bees have keepers. Asylums have keepers, and, as the terrible old joke said, zoos have keepers, too. But not our brother or sister! The one who tries to be the sister or brother's keeper often has that patronizing superiority that makes so much of our charity an offense against human dignity. It may be this implicit claim to superiority that makes the word *do-gooder* ring so foul in our ears. That, by the way, is the point of Riemann's fine essay, that we should avoid the arrogance of thinking that we are keepers of other human beings.

Let us lay aside this text for a moment and simply ask a straightforward general question: Who according to the Bible is the keeper of human beings? We can scarcely put the question into words without immediately knowing the answer. There is but one true "keeper" in the Bible: "The LORD is your keeper. . . . He who keeps Israel will neither slumber nor sleep" (Ps. 121:4-5); "The LORD bless you and keep you" (Num. 6:24).

Let me make a methodological observation here. In my book *Preaching that Matters*, I have argued that we can profitably search for and structure our sermons around analogies between figures or groups in the text and figures and groups in our world. But I sometimes have difficulty teaching my students the difference between analogy and example. Some students look at these figures or groups with a view to finding either exemplary or reprehensible moral behavior in them. When we use the figures of the scriptures only as examples, moralism almost inevitably creeps in. It may be positive moralizing. Be brave like David. Be faithful like Abraham, or even dedicate yourselves to our building project like Nehemiah. It may be negative moralizing. Don't be cruel and heartless like Cain. It is, nevertheless, still moralizing. Old John Calvin was right when he said the law was like a mirror. It is better to use the figures and groups in our texts as a mirror in which we can catch sight of something in ourselves.

What do we see when we hold up Cain's question not as horrible example of indifference, but as a mirror? We should note first of all that this part of our story is, in effect, a trial. In that trial, Cain attempts to assert his innocence. His question to God must be understood as part of that attempt. It can best be understood as a rhetorical question. A person normally only asks a rhetorical question, especially in a trial, if both parties know and agree on the answer to the question. Clearly Cain only asks the question because he believes the answer to be no, and, furthermore, he expects God to answer the question the same way. We at least ought to consider the possibility that Cain is right. Given the evidence both positive and negative, brought forth by Riemann about the biblical understanding of "keeper," that Cain is not the keeper is a good deal more than a possibility.

Let us pause for another moment here. This story might be considered not only a trial, but also the world's oldest murder mystery. Given God's question, it could rightly be called a "whodunit." We are at present in verse 9 of 16, just halfway through our whodunit. Perhaps "whodunit" is an insufficiently theological and scholarly description of this tale, but, at the very least, it is a story. The genuine key point, the true climax of a story, does not usually occur at its halfway point. "Am I my brother's keeper?" only becomes a key point if the interpreter is reading the story with the intent of discovering a starting point for a moral discourse. It may not be so vital if we go to the text not to seek a hook on which to hang our moral instruction, but rather to see signs of the grace of God to which we preachers are called to bear witness, to reach for rainbows. (The actual murder could be the starting point of a moral discourse, but to a generally nonhomicidal audience, "Do not murder" is a less compelling point than "Be your sister or brother's keeper." This assumes, of course, that most of our congregations are nonhomicidal.)

The real reason we ought not to rush to hang our moral instruction on Cain's question is that to do so blinds us to its theological depth. Perhaps Cain is a better theologian than the preachers. Perhaps he does know who is his brother's keeper. In the flow of the story, his question functions as a challenge and indeed as an implicit rebuke to God. It is as if he were saying, "Am I my brother's keeper? No, you are, and you are not carrying out your role properly. If something evil has happened to my brother, it is your failure."

All this raises the question of God's responsibility for evil, anticipated already in Eve's words "with the help of the Lord." Rabbi Gunther Plaut puts it bluntly: "Cain asks the Auschwitz question."[12] Why is God not a better keeper? Why does God allow innocent blood to fall to the ground, not just in this story, but again and again and again? Plaut tells us that this is not a new understanding of Cain's question. An ancient rabbi, Shimon bar Yochai, when commenting on this passage, recognized that God, by not acting to preserve Abel, had permitted his murder. In a strange and puzzling analogy, Rabbi Shimon even compared God to an emperor deliberately choosing to allow two gladiators to battle to the death.[13]

The "Auschwitz question" remains painfully unanswerable. But the Auschwitz question is one thing when it is asked by a death camp prisoner. It is quite another thing when it is asked by the death camp commandant. Cain's question is more like the latter. Cain blames God for his own evil. When we hold Cain up as a mirror, we see something very similar in ourselves. Do we not often blame God for our own evil? The question of theodicy is an enormous one. For Christians, there can be no answer, not even a provisional one, short of the cross. But there is another question, perhaps more pressing in our congregations than "Why does God let evil happen?" It is "Why do we let evil happen?"

There is a story that finds its way into many sermons, about Mother

Teresa challenged by a skeptical reporter. The reporter points to the misery of human life, speaks of a child dying alone in a Calcutta alley, and asks, "Where was God?" And Mother Teresa replied, "Where were you?" Perhaps only a very great saint can ask such a pointed question. Someone we love dies of a lingering, incurable illness, and we lament bitterly, asking rightly, for lament and complaint against God is often right, "Why did you allow this to happen?" But in the time our loved one has been wasting away, millions die of hunger, and we have known the cure for hunger for quite some time. Moreover, inasmuch as they die because of the systems from which we profit, the question may not be only "Why do we let evil happen?" It might be "Why do we make evil happen?" We are not called to be our brother's keeper, but that is no reason to let or to make our sister or brother die in misery.

"Am I my brother's keeper?" we ask. Perhaps we have inherited not only Cain's taste for violence, but his effrontery and hypocrisy as well.

But the blood cries out from the ground. This may be a first opportunity to see grace in the story, even if only by way of contrast. Sydney Greidanus, in a recent book *Preaching Christ from the Old Testament*, argues that we may do just that—preach the grace of Christ by contrast with some aspect of the Old Testament text.[14] The author of the letter to the Hebrews makes just such a move, calling us to faith in Jesus, the mediator of a new covenant and in "the sprinkled blood that speaks a better word than the blood of Abel" (Heb. 12:24). But perhaps there is a word of hope and grace for us here even without the move to the blood of Christ. Our pain, our suffering and sorrow cry out to the God of heaven, and God hears. God hears our troubles and takes action to rescue us. At the very least, it is assertion of the justice of God.

There is truth in this understanding. But it is a very limited truth. The problem is that if we make this move, we are identifying with Abel. When wrong is done to us, we cry out, and God hears. But it would be wiser by far to identify with Cain. In the first place, Cain, not Abel, is the main human character in the story, and interpreters should always deal first with those who are center stage in these dramas. Moreover, the text reminds us in a profound psychological insight that there are many descendants of Cain (Gen. 4:17ff.). Cain is our great grandfather. The blood cries out against us.

We are not innocent bystanders amidst the blood and carnage of the world and ought not to pretend otherwise. With all our wishful thinking, we cannot pretend otherwise. The blood does cry out, but it cries out against us, against our wealth and our lifestyle. This is not comforting; indeed, it ought to be terrifying, for according to our text, *God hears.*

At this point, it must be noted, we are still not preaching grace. We may be preaching justice, and preaching justice is always worthwhile. Indeed, preaching justice is "meet, right and our bounden duty." It would, however, be the subject of another book, though I will briefly address the subject in a later chapter. But it is terribly easy for the preaching of justice to become merely another form of tedious moralizing harangue. Please do not misunderstand this. If we do not preach justice, we are violating the will of God. But equally, if we preach justice that is separated from grace, we are likewise violating that will.

So back to the story. The trial now reaches its climax. The devastating and incriminating evidence has been introduced. Cain is found guilty, and sentence is pronounced. The punishment does fit the crime: "And now you are cursed from the ground, which has opened its mouth to receive your brother's blood from your hand. When you till the ground, it will no longer yield to you its strength; you will be a fugitive and a wanderer on the earth."

Once again, there is an echo of the sentence on Adam. History already repeats itself. The severing of right relationship with the other also damages the relationship with earth itself.

Cain protests the severity of the sentence: "My punishment is greater than I can bear!" He even fears that "anyone who meets me may kill me." There may be a small preaching problem here. A literalist of a skeptical bent may ask, "Who is around who might kill Cain?" A different literalist might reply that in a fratricidal world, Cain might eventually be threatened by Seth, whose birth is described later in the chapter, or by Seth's descendants. But in a sermon, it is probably best simply to stay within the story and concentrate on the story's concerns. By doing so, the preacher models a more imaginative stance with respect to the text. In any case, the trial is over. The verdict has been rendered and the sentence passed. "Guilty!"

VERSES 13-16, THE MARK OF CAIN

Within the story, the Lord responds to Cain's fear by placing a mark on him. We might think of the "mark of Cain" as some brand of shame or punishment, something like the scarlet letter in Nathaniel Hawthorne's novel. After all, one biblical Greek word for *mark* has passed into our language, *stigma*. We might think of the mark on Cain as a stigma. We might also think of the mark of the beast in the book of Revelation. And here, surprisingly enough, we would both be and not be "near the mark." We would be wrong if we think that the mark is a mark of rejection. But we would be nearly right if we remembered that the mark of the beast is a mark of ownership. This is something we ought to be able to understand.

Marks on the skin, tattoos, have made a tremendous comeback in recent years. For the most part, these marks indicate if not ownership, at least affiliation. A tattoo may show that we belong to a gang or a regiment or a nation or perhaps just "Mother." Those bearing the mark of the beast belong to the beast.

But Cain bears God's mark. It is also perfectly possible to bear a mark that shows that one belongs to God. So in the strange vision of Ezekiel 9, a "man clothed in linen" is called to go through the doomed city of Jerusalem and "put a mark on the foreheads of those who sigh and groan over all the abominations that are committed in it" (Ezek. 9:4). Then there is the awful command, "Cut down old men, young men and young women, little children and women, but touch no one who has the mark. And begin at my sanctuary" (Ezek. 9:6). Those with the mark are to be spared like Cain. Or in the new Jerusalem, the heavenly city, we read: "But the throne of God and of the Lamb will be in it, and his servants will worship him; they will see his face, and his name will be on their foreheads" (Rev. 22:3-4). In the same manner, the murderer is marked not for destruction, but for deliverance: "And the LORD put a mark on Cain, so that no one who came upon him would kill him."

But we have not yet "hit the mark," for we have not yet considered the actual word in Genesis 4:15, *oth*. It's a word that is usually translated not as *mark* but as *token, pledge,* or *sign.* It is even sometimes used of miracles, which are signs in the Bible of the presence and power of God. The saving blood of the Passover is such a sign (Exod. 12:13). A child born to a young woman who will call him Immanuel (Isa. 7:14) is a sign. There is even another appearance of the word very near our story in the primeval history of the book of Genesis. It can be found in Genesis 9: "I have set my bow in the clouds, and it shall be a *sign* of the covenant between me and the earth. . . . When the bow is in the clouds, I will see it and remember the everlasting covenant between God and every living creature of all flesh that is on the earth" (Gen. 9:13, 16).

We have reached for a rainbow and found one on Cain. God lays claim to the bloodstained murderer and makes him safe.

CONCLUSION: PREACHING GRACE FROM GENESIS 4

Perhaps we have now come near not just to a rainbow, but to the cross and to the table that points to the cross. That is a move that is probably not acceptable in a paper for the academic guild of biblical scholars. But if we are preaching in a Christian setting and, particularly, if we are preaching before a celebration of the Eucharist, the move may not only be permitted, but almost required. (The preacher's task is like that of the headwaiter, to say to Christ's guests, "Right this way, his table's waiting."[15])

Within the canon of Scripture as a whole, which for Christians centers in the gracious work of God in Jesus Christ, one may rightly hear analogies of grace among the parts of Scripture. So if we look and listen for grace in our text, we will find it, even "the grace of our Lord Jesus Christ." We will hear the cry of the blood of another brother unjustly slain. That blood does in truth cry out against my sin and the sin of an uncaring and violent world. We dare not evade that truth even when listening for grace. But that blood also cries out for mercy. By that mercy, as a camel passes through the eye of a needle, as we pass through fire, with great difficulty we may be saved. We do not now claim to stand like the redeemed in the New Jerusalem, marked with the name of the Lord. But through grace we are marked like Cain, but with the blood of the lamb. And that mark is grace, all grace.

CHAPTER 9

2 Kings 5:1-14 (15-27): And None Was Healed Except Naaman

This is not one of the best-known stories of the Old Testament; Noah's ark, Moses in the bulrushes, or David and Goliath fills that bill. My children had Noah's ark toys and even bedsheets when they were little, but nobody is going to get rich making "healing of Naaman" products. It is, however, hardly a passage that should lie in obscurity. According to the Gospel of Luke, Jesus referred to it in his first sermon in his hometown synagogue (Luke 4:27). Contemporary preachers might well imitate the master with profit, for this too is a great text.

At least this story, unlike the old tale of Cain and Abel, makes it into the new canon, the Revised Common Lectionary. To be more exact, half the story (vv. 1-14) makes it into the lectionary. The prescribed reading tells us only part of the strange story. The part we read in church seems a cheerful, at times nearly comic, tale of a miracle.[1] The story as a whole carries a more pointed and profound message. The preacher might want to carry on in the sermon where the lectionary leaves off and complete the story for the listeners. Other readers will be more closely bound by church law or tradition or simply by the constraints of time to the lectionary as it stands. A faithful sermon or homily may grow from the part of the passage actually prescribed by the lectionary. Nevertheless, the text cannot be rightly understood unless the preacher considers the passage as a whole.

THE LITERARY CONTEXT

The Elisha Cycle

The text can also not be rightly understood apart from its literary context. It is part of the Deuteronomic history as a whole and of the Elisha cycle within that greater work. The Elisha cycle begins when Elisha picks up the mantle of the departed Elijah (2 Kings 2:13). It is marked by a series of miracles, some of which may be puzzling or even embarrassing to the contemporary reader. (One thinks in this connection particularly of the story of Elisha and the she-bears [2 Kings 2:23-25].) It should be noted, however, that a number of the miracle stories echo events of Israel's glorious salvation history. So, for example, Elisha parts the waters of the Jordan (2 Kings 2:14) and provides water in the wilderness (2 Kings 3:9-20). Some of these miracles also echo the work of his illustrious predecessor Elijah. So Elisha provides for a widow (2 Kings 4:1-8), as does Elijah (1 Kings 17:8-16). (Note the miraculous flow of oil in both stories.) Furthermore, Elisha raises a son to life (2 Kings 4:8-37), as Elijah had done (1 Kings 17:17-24). Elisha is presented in the narrative as a miracle worker and as one who stands within the classic traditions of Israel.

It is also worth noting that the storyteller is less than impressed by the king of Israel. The king in question is Jehoram, a son of Ahab and Jezebel. (He comes from a bad family.) "He did what was evil in the sight of the LORD, though not like his father and mother. . . . Nevertheless he clung to the sin of Jeroboam son of Nebat, which he caused Israel to commit; he did not depart from it" (2 Kings 3:2-3). The last phrase, of course, is the standard denunciation of the kings of Israel by the Deuteronomistic historian. There is something more (or perhaps less) with the portrait of Jehoram, however. Jehoram chooses to invade rebellious Moab in company with the kings of both Judah and Edom by way of the wilderness of Edom (2 Kings 3:4-27). Within a week, the armies have run out of water on his chosen route and may have to surrender ignominiously to Moab. Surely the reader knows that only a very incompetent general would get an army into such a fix. In that dire situation, Jehoram at last wants to turn to a prophet. But he does not even know if a prophet has accompanied the expedition, a sign, doubtless, of the depth of his devotion to the Lord. It is a servant who knows of Elisha's presence (2 Kings 3:11), a motif we shall see again in our passage.

Elisha, when summoned, is direct in his scorn, "Go to your father's prophets or to your mother's" (2 Kings 3:13). But when begged to act, he finally accedes. It is clear, however, that his estimate of Jehoram has not changed: "As the LORD of hosts lives, whom I serve, were it not that I have regard for King Jehoshaphat of Judah, I would give you neither a look nor a glance" (2 Kings 3:14). So much for the king of Israel! Nor will he, though he has witnessed a miracle that echoes the ancient stories of the preservation of Israel in the wilderness, be an impressive figure in our text.

One further observation might be made. If the Elisha cycle repeats themes from the Elijah cycle, we might in time read of a mighty work done for a Gentile (cf. 1 Kings 17:8-24). It is, of course, precisely this pattern that Jesus notes in the Nazareth sermon.

In summary, the Elisha cycle of stories has already anticipated certain motifs that we may find in the Naaman story. Elisha is primarily a miracle worker. The storyteller is not particularly respectful toward the rich and powerful. The king of Israel is an idiot. Finally, given the obvious parallels to the Elijah cycle, we ought not to be overly surprised if a Gentile shows up.

The Deuteronomistic History

Our story is not merely a part of a cycle of Elisha stories. It is also part of the Deuteronomist's great history of the people of Israel. In many ways, the latter part of this history is a sad and tragic one. The history begins in the book of Deuteronomy with the people of Israel hearing the words of the aged Moses before they pour with strength and violence into the land of Canaan. It ends with a people exiled from that land. Some have been dragged off into exile in Babylon. Others, after a tawdry and useless assassination of a collaborator, have fled back to the Egypt from whence the people had come in the beginning of the history. Of them we hear nothing more. There are, however, two signs of hope no bigger than a man's hand. The first can be found in the final words of the history, a strange little note concerning the rightful king Jehoiachin. In the thirty-seventh year of his exile, he has been released from captivity and is treated with honor. This suggests that whatever future belongs to Israel will be found with the exiles and with those who recognize the futility of resistance but will nevertheless struggle to live faithfully under the foreign yoke. The second sign of hope is this: Somebody is collecting and writing down the stories of Israel. That person or that circle of persons is able to trace the working of God's hand even through this tragic history of unfaithfulness. It may not be unduly speculative to imagine that the first audience for this story can be found among the exiles in Babylon, oppressed by Gentile power but, if rightly encouraged, able to trust in a power greater still, the God of Israel. The story of Naaman ought to be read with those exiles always in mind.[2]

Scene I: In Syria, 2 Kings 5:1-5a

This passage is a story, and its theological meaning will be conveyed in the strands of the narrative. One strand is nearly comic. The powerful in the story are represented as absurd and foolish figures. The most absurd figure of all is Naaman himself. As we shall see, the story all but ridicules him. As the story begins, however, Naaman is anything but a figure of fun. Rather, he is a celebrity, the kind of person whose house might be featured on *Lifestyles of the Rich and Famous*. But perhaps it would be better to put it in ancient rather than contemporary terms. Naaman is a Gentile, a victorious general held in high esteem by his master, the King of Aram (or Syria, as it is often called), Israel's unneighborly neighbor to the north. It is sadly ironic to note that Israel and Syria got along as well in those days as in ours. The preacher might want to continue the Middle East theme and call Naaman the "Stormin' Norman" Schwarzkopf of the ancient Middle East, the most successful general around and most certainly a VIP. The king of Aram probably thought that all that military success was due to Naaman, and Naaman might have shared that opinion. The Deuteronomist tells us this is not so, however. One would never expect God to work in favor of a foreigner, but so it is: "By him [Naaman] the LORD had given victory to Aram" (v. 1). This apparent throwaway line may have been as important as the healing for the first listeners. The King and Naaman and anybody else who supposes that the powerful control history are wrong. Their opinions need correcting, and perhaps that is just what will happen in our story.

Naaman, despite his triumphs, has leprosy. Note the contrast between his success and his sickness. Many skin conditions other than leprosy proper—the modern Hansen's disease—could have been labeled leprosy in the ancient world. The Good News Bible may have been wise when it labeled this condition simply "a dreaded skin disease." As such, he is not only a Gentile, but also ritually unclean, doubly distanced, one might suppose, from the God of Israel. For the sake of the story, the chief point about the illness is that it is beyond human cure. No one, not all the king's horses and all the king's men, not even the king himself, can do anything about it. The narrator lays out a dreadful contrast between human power and wealth, on the one hand, and complete impotence in the face of sickness and trouble, on the other. This is a contrast to be noted by the preacher because equivalent sorts of contrasts are common in our world too. Naaman, great general though he is, cannot command good health for himself. In fact, Naaman might not even be fully in charge of his own house.

It is at this point that the second strand in the story is introduced. In contrast to the absurdity of the great men throughout this story is the sensible behavior of the servants, both the Israelite slave girl and those who accompany Naaman to Elisha's home. We begin, however, with an Israelite slave girl. One commentator calls her a "stereotypical" character.[3] It may be that we do not have enough literature from the period to determine what a stereotypical character might actually be. But if we imagine for the moment that a serving girl with a heart of gold might have been a stock character twenty-five hundred years ago, we must still recognize the genuine theological seriousness of her role. One of Naaman's victims, an Israelite servant girl captured in the slave raids, is the agent of good news in the story. (Note that she too is an exile.) She might be expected to hate her captor, but she does not. The girl cares even when she has good reason not to. She tells her mistress of the astonishing power of a prophet in Samaria, not even named at this point. Quite obviously, Naaman's wife passed on the recommendation.

One cannot tell if the narrator wants the reader to think of the old story of Moses and the bulrushes here, but the connection now seems inescapable. In that familiar tale, Pharoah decreed that all the boy babies of the Hebrews should be slaughtered. The infant Moses was cast adrift in a tiny cradle of bulrushes. Pharaoh's daughter, as it happens, rescues him. Moses' sister likewise happens to be standing by, and she mentions that there happens to be a Hebrew woman who can nurse the child. Perhaps we readers might reasonably imagine that Pharaoh's daughter knew exactly what was going on here. She might be expected to hate those who are different, but she does not choose to hate. In that ancient tale, there is a "conspiracy" of women who know just what they want. What they want is humane and loving, no matter what the kings and the generals may say. Once again in our story, as with the tale of Moses and the bulrushes, powerless and powerful women combine to effect the will of God.

There is a potential preaching point here. The will of God is done not just in the clash of armies, but in the quiet concern of faithful and loving women and, for that matter, men, too. The world as we experience it and very likely as the exiles in Babylon experience it might say, "Look at the kings and the generals or at their VIP equivalents!" The Bible says, "Look for the quiet loving people who are doing God's will. They're the ones who matter."

Scene II: At the Court of the King of Israel, 2 Kings 5:5b-8

Naaman is granted permission by his king to seek healing among the enemy. The king of Aram, as one might expect, does what powerful men do. He sends with Naaman a letter to the king of Israel.[4] Naaman also takes a huge fortune in gifts to buy the cooperation of the prophet. Note how these great men operate: They live in a world of wealth and personal influence and automatically think that these things can procure healing. The reader of the book of Kings already knows that such attitudes are foolish, and we who listen now know it also. If we know anything about the Bible, even if we play the power and influence game the rest of the week, we know that this is not the way it works with God.

The letter is even more foolish. It begs the king of Israel, asking him to "cure him of his leprosy." "You!" not God. But the reader knows that no mere king can cure. The king of Israel also knows this. He even reminds us indirectly who does have the power, "Am I God, to give death or life?" But this is hardly a confession of faith. He too lives in the so-called great world of affairs and suspects that the Arameans are only using this request as an opportunity to pick an unequal fight. The picture of the king rending his garments in his terror is almost funny because he doesn't know what to do. At the very least we are meant to think once again, "How absurd these great men are in their pretensions."

The prophet must actually remind the king of his presence. The reader, whether ancient or contemporary, who has been told of Elisha's miracles in previous chapters will know that this is yet another royal absurdity. A slave girl up in Syria knows who can heal, but not the king of Israel! Note that we are invited again and again to think ill of the powerful in this story. The Bible doesn't seem to rate VIPs very highly. Who let these people write stories that show so little respect to the top people?

Scene III: The Prophet's House and the Jordan, 2 Kings 5:9-14

In due course, Naaman arrives with all the trappings of success, the horses and the chariots. The preacher might want to name a contemporary equivalent, perhaps a Mercedes stretch limo with motorcycle outriders. Certainly in our culture in which people bow down not in the House of Rimmon, but in the cult of celebrity, this would make quite a splash. It doesn't matter, however, to Elisha who doesn't even bother coming to the door. He sends his prescription by messenger: "Go wash in the Jordan seven times . . . and you shall be clean." The refusal to see Naaman and the simplicity of the remedy required are implicit statements about his relative importance in God's eyes compared to his awe-inspiring position in society. Naaman does take the point of this implied insult, but his petulant, nationalistic response is reported in such a way as to ridicule him even further in the eyes of the reader.

"I thought that for me he would surely come out, and stand and call on the name of the LORD his God, and would wave his hand over the spot, and cure the leprosy!" He wants a little respect and a performance. VIPs think they are entitled to a performance, of course, and they always deserve respect, especially if they show up at the door with the ancient version of a motorcade and a medium-sized fortune in gifts. It's hard even to describe Naaman's own performance without mockery, but mockery is doubtless exactly what the narrator wants from us. We often read the Bible aloud in church with stained-glass voices as if holiness and humor could never join together to the glory of God. It would be a mistake, however, to take or to read Naaman's words seriously. We are supposed to laugh aloud at this great general and his expectations. The balloon of his vanity has been pricked, and his words are just the hot air escaping.

For Naaman, patriotism is the last refuge of the bruised ego: "Are not Abana and Pharpar, the rivers of Damascus, better than all the waters of Israel? Could I not wash in them, and be clean?" We readers might echo Shakespeare at this point, "What fools these mortals be!" This may be especially the case if the mortals in question are rich and powerful and actually depend on their wealth and power for their salvation. So Naaman turns away from his healing "in a rage." Perhaps that may be too dignified a translation. Perhaps here the Hebrew might be rendered "in a snit."

Having thoroughly established the absurdity of the powerful, the narrator now brings back into view the other strand of the story, the role of the servants. The servants are quick-witted and tactful in their dealings with their enraged master. In contrast to their offended lord, they have at least an ounce or two of common sense. "If the prophet had commanded you to do something difficult, would you not have done it?" Why not just try what the prophet asks? And Naaman, according to the story, does as they ask and is healed.

PREACHING GRACE FROM 2 KINGS 5:1-14

At this point we have reached the climax of the story as it appears in the lectionary and as, to be realistic, it will usually be preached. A pause for homiletical reflection may therefore be in order. It may be particularly useful at this point to reflect on the situation of those for whom these old stories of Israel's past were first collected. Preachers will doubtless need to remind listeners that this was, to put it very mildly, a bad time for God's people. The foreign generals, in other words, the Naamans, had been far too successful. The city of Jerusalem had been captured, the walls torn down and the temple destroyed. Many of the Jews had been dragged off like the servant girl in our story, but to a place farther away than Naaman's house. They were exiles in Babylon, captives as in the long gone days of Moses and the Pharaoh. We know at least one of their songs of sorrow: "By the rivers of Babylon—there we sat down and there we wept when we remembered Zion" (Ps. 137:1). While they sang this ancient version of the blues, they watched. They saw the wealthy and the powerful with their horses and chariots. They saw great men who believed that they themselves ordered their lives with their power and influence.

The preacher might help the congregation picture these things and then imagine what the exiles needed. Perhaps, given the story to this point, it would be possible to suggest some answers. Perhaps the exiles needed to be reminded that servants and slaves sometimes know a truth that escapes their masters. They needed to be reminded who was really in charge. They needed to know that their God reigned. They even needed to be able to laugh at the VIPs parading in their "motorcades" through the streets of Babylon. But just when the listeners must have been feeling really, really good about themselves, just when they must have been glorying in their superiority to the rich and the powerful and to Gentiles in general, something surprising happens.

"Why not do what the prophet says?" say Naaman's servants, and they wheedle him into trying. So he does what the prophet says. There happens the very thing such a ridiculous figure manifestly does not deserve: He is healed.

Perhaps a dose of reality is in order here. This book is written by a Canadian and published by an American press. Most readers will be citizens of wealthy and powerful nations, for the most part, in fact, of the "world's sole remaining superpower." We may not be famous, but by the standards of the wider world, we are indeed rich. The primary market for this book is not made up of the contemporary equivalents of exiles. The story may have been written for captives far from home. It is now to be preached in congregations at home amidst wealth and power. In some churches the equivalent of Naaman may even be sitting in the third pew from the back. The story was not written for us; at best we listen in on it. In the story it's a surprise that grace reaches Naaman. We can see that if we read the story rightly. A very real problem with preaching grace is simply this; it is no longer all that surprising. Many of us who have sung "Amazing Grace" all our lives take it as a matter of course that grace should come to us. If we really are more like Naaman than like the exiles, it still should be a surprise that grace can reach us. That reality can be preached even from a truncated version of the story.

2 Kings 5:15-19a, Naaman Responds to the Healing

These verses do not constitute a new scene in the story as a whole. Rather, they are a continuation of the previous scene. The interaction between Naaman and Elisha falls naturally into three subunits: Elisha's house—the Jordan—Elisha's house. We have reached the third of those subunits. The slight break at this point partially justifies the decision of the framers of the lectionary to cut the text at this point. One suspects, however, that the decision to shorten the text was based on liturgical and practical rather than exegetical grounds. Though the lectionary reading ends, the interaction between the prophet and Naaman does not. The preacher ought to study the remainder of the text even if little or none of this material makes its way into the sermon.

In response to the healing, Naaman, seemingly a changed man, offers a moving confession of faith: "Now I know that there is no God in all the earth except in Israel." This confession has been anticipated earlier in the story. At this moment, Naaman grasps what the narrator has already told us in verse 1. It is the Lord who is sovereign over human affairs. It is also a completion of the inadequate confession implied by the words of the king of Israel, "Am I God, to give death or life?" (v. 7). One might expect this confession would be the climax of the story. The story could end here with this ringing declaration of monotheism. Something like this, after all, is what a man healed by the grace of God is supposed to say. How beautiful, edifying, and unsurprising such a conclusion would be. And how easily it would preach!

The narrator keeps surprising us, however. Naaman continues his speech with an offer of a gift to the prophet. We have considered Naaman a figure of fun throughout this passage, but there is nothing to be ridiculed here. It is indeed right that grace should evoke gratitude. There is a certain dignity in Naaman's behavior at this point. It is, on the other hand, also appropriate and not at all surprising that Elisha should refuse the gift. Grace does not have a price, even a post-event price. One of the narrative functions of the offer, we may note, is that it sets up the final episode of the story as a whole.

There follows an interchange that may seem nearly incomprehensible to the contemporary interpreter, but may well have been of first importance in the original setting. It begins with Naaman's notion that it would be helpful to have two mule loads of Israelite dirt back home. Presumably he wants to pray or to offer sacrifice on this soil. Behind the request seems to be the belief that the power of a god was linked to a particular location. It is possible to understand this request, obviously misguided though it is, in a positive light. Perhaps Naaman was "planting the flag behind enemy lines." Perhaps this was a "beachhead" of monotheism in a pagan land. If, however, we keep in mind the situation for which the text was written and if we remember the way in which the narrator has tended to ridicule Naaman, another interpretation suggests itself.

Perhaps this part of the story might have evoked an internal dialogue in the first listeners/readers in their Babylonian exile:

Listener: "He wants two loads of Israelite dirt."

Text: "Perhaps he thinks the Lord's power is tied to the soil."

Listener: "That's ridiculous! As if God's power could be geographically limited!"

Text: "So if God's power is not confined to the soil of Israel, why are you weeping by the waters of Babylon as if the hand of the Lord could never reach you there?"

Though the dialogue may seem fanciful, the intent to have the listener draw a conclusion appropriate to the situation of the exile does not.

There then follows the dialogue concerning bowing down with Naaman's master in the temple of Rimmon. One might expect that the Deuteronomic historian, who largely blames the disasters that have befallen Israel and Judah upon their indulgence in idolatry, would clearly declare than no form of idolatry is acceptable under any circumstances. Once again the text surprises us. No answer whatsoever is given. Perhaps this reflects a genuine sensitivity to the compromises the exiles must make in an indifferent or even hostile setting. We might note, however, that the Deuteronomistic historian is not noticeably tolerant toward the Baal worshipers of Israel (cf. 2 Kings 10:18-31). It seems more likely, therefore, that the narrator is continuing, though more gently, the mockery of Naaman. The very name *Rimmon* might be a clue here. Though the word sounds like a title of a particular Syrian Baal, it actually means "pomegranate" in Hebrew. One might compare this to the way a person of anti-American tendencies might make "United States" into "Untied" States or "Benighted" States. Naaman's god is of no more use than a pomegranate. To worship such a "god" is absurd. In the end, Elisha won't even answer Naaman's question. In truth, given what we read in 1 and 2 Kings, no answer is needed, if the question were taken seriously. But perhaps the question is not taken seriously in the story. What, after all, could one actually say to a character such as Naaman? Perhaps all that can or need be said is "shalom," in an amused voice.

Scene IV: Gehazi's Greed, 2 Kings 5:19b-27

At this point we come to the concluding episode of the story as a whole. It is virtually self-explanatory and needs little exposition here. Older commentators sometimes speculated that this was an addition to the original story. Whether or not that is the case, it fits neatly at this point. It has been anticipated by Elisha's refusal to take a gift (v. 15), and it tidily rounds off the story as a whole. The conniving servant is afflicted with the very disease of which Naaman had been cured.

There is, however, an element of surprise in this concluding episode. To this point, the literary pattern of the story has been consistent. The rich and powerful are ridiculed, and the servants are portrayed as wise, sensible, and caring. Now suddenly the powerful man acts with dignity and the servant is shown to be dishonest. Though Naaman may be mocked, he may not be robbed. The powerful need not be taken seriously, but they must not be just "taken." The eventual punishment certainly fits the crime.[5]

CONCLUSION: PREACHING GRACE FROM THE STORY OF NAAMAN

It appears to be the literary strategy of the narrator to catch the listener or reader by surprise. We might ask ourselves what surprise this tale of the healing of a foreign general would have for exiles. Surely there would be great enjoyment in the depiction of the folly of the upper crust and the cleverness of the servants. There is more here, however, than the simple-minded reversal that both ancient and contemporary hearers might relish. The story is told in a nearly comic vein, but it makes a serious point. God's mercy must always be taken seriously. Moreover, that mercy is not confined to Israel or even to the powerless. No wonder this passage is mentioned in a certain sermon in Nazareth, Luke 4:16-30.

The strategy of reversal may actually continue to work for preachers who belong to the so-called mainline Christian traditions. Most of us who have been educated in those traditions have been exposed to a greater or lesser degree to liberation thinking and its preferential option for the poor. To us, as to the exiles, it seems right and proper that God should work through the servants. We too are ready to hear a story in which the mighty are ridiculed and the poor praised and lifted up. All this seems to us theologically correct. Just when we think we understand how the story is working, however, it surprises us. It tricks us into looking down on the powerful foreigner, and then, suddenly and without repentance, he is healed. Furthermore, the story ends with Elisha's Israelite servant trying to defraud the scorned foreigner. The punishment fits the crime; the servant is stricken by the leprosy that formerly afflicted Naaman. The story is in the end about the sovereignty of God whose grace is so surprising that it reaches even the ridiculous.

We might be tempted to suppose that the grace of God works and should always work as a favor shown to those on the underside of life. But such an understanding would make grace predictable. This story, whatever else it says about grace, denies us the right to suppose that grace is ever predictable.

The Bible invites us to live in a strange new world. Obviously, it is a world in which power and personal influence and vast sums of money do not rule and in which the VIPs who have these things deserve scant respect. That makes it different from the world we live in most of the time. It is a world in which the servants and the slaves and the down-trodden can be agents of God's mercy and grace while kings and gener-als look like fools. But just when you think you understand the rules for grace, you get fooled. Even the rich and the powerful can be touched by mercy.

Maybe there are no rules for grace, even theologically correct ones. Maybe it is just there when we least expect it.

CHAPTER 10

Psalm 119:
The Law As Gospel

A visit to the collected sermons section of a theological library will demonstrate that our ancestors in the faith preached regularly from the Psalms. Preaching from the Psalms may not be as common today, however, particularly among those who follow the Revised Common Lectionary. There is a widespread assumption that we ought to preach primarily from the Gospel lesson for the day and if not from the Gospel, then from the Old Testament or Epistle. It is even claimed by some that we *ought not* to preach from the Psalms in that these are the words of the community to God rather than God's word to us. I cannot debate this dubious claim here. I will only say that in the Psalms we often witness the divine/human encounter at its most touching, problematic, and profound point. To ignore the Psalms in our preaching is to cut ourselves off homiletically from one of the greatest spiritual resources of Israel and the church. The question under consideration here is not whether it is possible to preach from the Psalms, but how to preach *grace* from the Psalms.

It would, in fact, be relatively easy to preach grace from many Psalms. Think, for example, of Psalm 136, with its celebration of the God who has acted in creation and in redemptive history. Hear its repeated refrain: "For his steadfast love endures forever." The psalm is a litany of grace. It would also be easy to preach grace from the much loved psalm of the shepherd whose rod and staff give comfort even in the valley of the shadow of death. It would even be easy to preach from the psalm that begins in despair, "My God, my God, why have you forsaken me?" but ends in praise. It would be far more difficult, however, to preach grace from other psalms, from psalms that call for God to wreak vengeance on the enemy or that declare at length the psalmist's own innocence. It might, at first sight, also seem difficult to preach grace from the seemingly endlessly repeated encomiums of the law of God in Psalm 119. We Christians are disposed to think that if there is anything in the religion of the Old Testament that is the *antithesis* of the gospel of free grace, it is surely the law of God. We say "law and gospel" in the same way we say "black and white" or "happy and sad." They are, in our mind, opposites.

The matter must not be left to rest here, however. The risen Christ made not only the prophets, but also the law to speak of him on the Emmaus Road. And their hearts burned within them when they heard his teaching. Rightly understood, the law of God still points to that grace that we Christians see in Jesus Christ.

There are both social and theological reasons, however, that cause us to preach only reluctantly about the law of God. In the first place, there is in our society a deep ambivalence toward the very concept of law. It is certainly true that we are intensely litigious. It is said, for example, that there are more lawyers in the Los Angeles area than in the nation of France. If we perceive we have suffered a wrong, from the temperature of the coffee at a fast food restaurant to the pain of childbirth,[1] it seems to us that the law should fix it. We appear to expect the operation of the law to right all wrongs and ease all pain. One might at first think that our society is in love with law. But that is not the whole picture. When legislatures enact regulations, often in response to our pleas and designed in the first place to protect us, we complain bitterly about red tape. It may be that our society, though litigious, does not love the concept of law. We are profoundly individualistic and impatient of any restraints. In a setting of ambivalence toward the law of the state, is it very likely that we will easily value the law of God? In such a setting, the sheer, overflowing delight in the law of God that fills the 176 verses of Psalm 119 can at first seem, as C. S. Lewis wrote, "utterly bewildering."[2] It is by no means easy to preach the law of God.

The most difficult problem in dealing with Psalm 119 and compositions like it is, however, a theological one. We spiritual descendants of the apostle Paul often appear to live with a sharp distinction between law and gospel. We take as our theological touchstone some of the apostle's most polemical statements in the Epistle to the Galatians and do not read them in a wider canonical context, which can delight in law as a gift from God. We have, too often, lost our theological balance in this matter, and it shows in our preaching. It has been said that a society warns most sternly against those sins that it is least likely to commit. We regularly preach sermons on the evils of legalism, but when did we last hear a sermon warning against antinomianism? (Antinomianism is the opposite of legalism, a belief that, for those freed by grace, law no longer matters.) Even Paul paused, in the midst of his letter to the Galatians, to redress the balance and to recognize a positive and right use of the law. If our preaching is biblically and theologically balanced, we will have to deal with texts like Psalm 119 that praise the law of God.

The length and complex structure of the psalm also conspire to make this psalm in particular difficult preaching material. (A certain Puritan divine, however, reportedly preached 190 consecutive sermons on the psalm. They had stamina in those days!) One commentator, Artur Weiser, called Psalm 119 "a particularly artificial product of religious poetry."[3] As is well known, Psalm 119 is an acrostic psalm. Each successive eight-line strophe or section of the psalm begins with a particular letter of the Hebrew alphabet, in the order of the Hebrew alphabet. All the remaining lines of the strophe also begin with that letter. So the first strophe has eight lines, each a bicolon (a line with two approximately equal sections), beginning with the Hebrew letter *aleph,* the second strophe, with the let-ter *bet,* and so on. Eight key terms are repeated constantly through these strophes. These are torah/law, the key and comprehensive term, and the following: decrees, statutes, commandments, ordinances, word, precepts, and promise. This might be interesting material for the seminary course on the Psalms, but the homiletical usefulness of these observations is not immediately apparent. Perhaps it is not even particularly fascinating material for the seminary. Weiser also called the psalm a "mosaic of thoughts which are often repeated in a wearisome fashion."[4] Far more generous of spirit is James Luther Mays's claim that the psalmist "used the alphabet to signal completeness and the whole vocabulary to repre-sent comprehensiveness."[5]

Mays may have been more sympathetic than older commentators because he also recognized the essentially oral character of the psalm. This psalm was composed to be read or sung aloud. He suggests, there-fore, that the psalm ought to be read aloud to oneself or to others. To do so in worship might well try the patience of a contemporary congrega-tion. This is not primarily because of literary failure in the psalm. Many of the individual lines are extraordinarily beautiful and pithy and could easily be quoted in most of our churches. Rather, it is because the piety that animates the psalm, a piety of devotion to torah, is so rare among contemporary Christians. Even the Protestant equivalent of that piety, a piety of the Word of God, is becoming rarer, at least in the so-called main-line churches.

Nevertheless, Psalm 119 is indeed a great text. It appears more often in the Revised Common Lectionary than any other psalm. It has been in the past a favorite text of preachers. Most important, this text can give us not so much a doctrine of the law as an attitude to it that will allow us to see in the law as a whole not just the burdensome demands, but the grace of a loving God. It is impossible here to consider the psalm in its entirety. We shall consider, however, a representative sample of it.

Psalm 119:105-12

This eight-verse section of the psalm is composed of lines beginning with the Hebrew letter *nun,* the sound equivalent of *n* in our alphabet. By this stage of the psalm, the reader is thoroughly familiar with the vocabulary and style of the psalmist. If the psalm has "worked" for the readers or listeners, they have now been caught up in heart and mind into the delight in the law that suffuses the psalm as a whole.

Verses 105-106, Your Word Is a Lamp

The section begins with the most familiar verse in the entire psalm: "Your word is a lamp to my feet and a light to my path." The imagery is simple and powerful but perhaps too familiar to preach well. Many Christians who grew up in the days of memory work may know the verse by heart. What may seem foreign to Christians, however, is the fact that the "word" that guides our feet is the law. We live with a notion that the law of God is a burden, an impossibly high set of standards whose chief function is to show how far short we fall of the glory of God. In Psalm 119, however, the law is the beloved guide. The task of the preacher may not be to explain these words. They are, after all, easily comprehensible. Rather, our task is to refresh the imagery, a matter to which we shall return later. The word precisely in its capacity as guide is not simply a burden, but a blessing. It is the set of careful instructions for the journey written by one who knows the way. The wise consult these instructions at every turn. It is the flashlight we hold in our hands as we walk on a moonless night in the lonely countryside. The wise walk within its light and are thankful.

In response to this gift, the psalmist declares, "I have sworn an oath and confirmed it, to observe your righteous ordinances." The oath that is sworn and confirmed might best be understood as the equivalent of a public profession of faith in Christ. The depth of commitment here is similar in kind to that which evangelical Christians celebrate among those who have truly "committed their lives to Christ." It is as if the psalmist sings, "I have decided to follow . . . your gracious law. No turning back, no turning back."

Verses 107-110, I Am Severely Afflicted but Do Not Stray

Sensitive Christians may well fear the possibility of a self-righteousness that may come from a careful attention to the law's demands. There is, however, no self-righteousness here. The psalmist does not hold up the law and say, "See how I have observed your laws. Now reward me as I deserve." Rather, the psalmist turns to God in prayer. In a way, this small section of Psalm 119 is a microcosm of the psalter as a whole and of the psalms of lament in particular. First, there is the complaint that gives a lament its name: "I am severely afflicted." There then follows humble petition: "Give me life, O LORD, according to your word." We may note in this phrase that the word functions for the psalmist not just as guidance, but as promise. The central promise of Scripture as a whole, as this verse implies, is life. As in the psalter as a whole, there is also praise, the con-clusion of most psalms of lament: "Accept my offerings of praise, O LORD." These three elements—complaint, petition, and praise—are found in most laments (see, for example, Psalms 10, 22, 35). The easy way the psalmist moves among these categories suggests that there is no sharp distinction among them. The one guided by the light of the word is also the one who laments. Moreover, the one who laments is also, in the Psalms, the one who prays, who is rescued, and who offers praise.

The psalmist then circles back to the law as instruction: "and teach me your ordinances." The keeping of the law is not, as we might be tempted to think, a human achievement. Indeed, it cannot be learned apart from the teaching of God.

In verse 109, the psalmist returns to language reminiscent of the laments: "I hold my life in my hand continually." Some Christians, fear-ing any expression of self-sufficiency, might think it more properly pious to say, "You hold my life in your hands continually." Judging by the par-allelism with the following verse, the psalmist is not claiming control over his life, but referring to the uncertainty of a life threatened on all sides. Despite those threats, the psalmist does not forget God's law. Amidst the dangers and stresses of life, it might be easy to do so. Once again, it is clear that the "law" is not to the psalmist a series of impossi-ble or at least unpleasant burdens. What the law does mean and how to preach it is the subject of the next section of this chapter. At this point, we shall merely note that the law gives support and comfort if it is remem-bered when our lives are in our hands. "Forgetting" the law of God may mean, in this context, forgetting the sovereign love of God, which is made known to us not only in the "prophets" and above all in Jesus Christ, but also in the "law." The Torah also assures us that God is merciful and that a life lived in obedient and loving relationship with God is for our good.

The "wicked" make their appearance in many psalms and do so also in this psalter in miniature. It is characteristic of the wicked that they set snares (see, for example, Psalm 64:2-5 or Psalm 38:12: "Those who seek my life lay their snares"). It is because of the wicked that the life of the psalmist is threatened. It is also because of the snare of the wicked that we need so much guidance in life. Despite these snares, the psalmist promises not to stray from God's precepts. Straying from the precepts probably does not mean only being tempted to do some wrong that violates God's commandments. It is more likely that it means ceasing to trust, in our despair over the threats of the enemies, that it is God's will to order our lives through these precepts for our good. More simply, it may mean losing sight of the goodness of God as in, for example, Psalm 73.

Verses 111-112, the Joy of My Heart

"Your decrees are my heritage forever; they are the joy of my heart," says the psalmist. The words are easy to comprehend. The feeling behind them may be hard to grasp for Christians. In order to do so, we might ask ourselves what words are those to which we intend to cling all our lives. Which words do we intend to pass on to our children? Which words give us joy? For us, those words are probably the words of the gospel. The decrees of the law function for the psalmist in the way that those words function for us.

The heart was for the Hebrews, the seat not of the emotions, but of the will. It represents the fundamental orientation of one's life. To "incline my heart to perform your statutes forever, to the end" means to direct the whole of life to obedience. Obedience might sound burdensome and threatening in our ears. It is not; for the psalmist it is pure joy. As the psalmist will declare in the first line of the next section of the psalm, "I love your law." That which we love we turn to with joy.

PREACHING THE LAW AS GOSPEL

To preach the law as gospel is to declare the law not an intolerable burden, but rather a gift of the grace of God. The relationship of law and gospel has been since the days of the apostle Paul a vexed question for the Christian church. The problem reemerged strongly at the time of the Reformation, in large part because of the spiritual experience of Martin Luther. From his reading of Scripture, Luther came to believe with all his heart that we are justified by faith apart from the works of the law. If it is impossible to earn God's favor by fulfilling the law, is there any continuing use for the law for Christians? In some formulations, law became almost the antithesis of gospel. The word *law* became a code word for our vain attempts to please God by our own pitiful attempts at righteousness.

Christian theology has sometimes striven, however, to identify positive uses of the law. Paul himself identifies one relationship between law and gospel in Galatians 3:19-25. Law has a preparatory or "propadeutic" function with respect to the gospel. It is the "schoolmaster to Christ" or the "disciplinarian," as the NRSV renders the key term *paidogogos*. The picture here is of the slave who takes the small child safely to school, preserves the child from harm, and, when necessary, disciplines the child. (It is unfortunate that the NRSV took the most negative of the roles for its rendering of the Greek.) This is, as Paul notes in Galatians 4:1-7, a temporary state of affairs; it lasts only until the heir becomes an adult. Law, therefore, prepares the way for the gospel.

This view of the law has been immensely significant in many ways for preaching. It will express itself most naturally in a two-part sermon that moves from law to gospel. The law will generally function in the first half of these sermons as a "measuring stick," "hammer," or "mirror."[6] Much American Protestant preaching, particularly evangelistic preaching, appears to have used the law in this preparatory manner. The preacher uses the measuring stick of the law to show our human failure and our complete inability to please God by our own efforts. Sometimes, in cruder versions of such preaching, the preacher dwells on the terrifying consequences of our failure to "scare the hell out" of the listener. In such cases, the law is more hammer than measuring stick. After the law in these sermons comes the gospel. Once the listeners are awakened to their need by the law, the gospel is presented as the answer to that need. This movement may be handled crudely or with great sophistication, but it is pretty widely present in evangelistic preaching.

There is, however, a preparatory use of the law that is neither measuring stick nor hammer. This manner of using the law is extremely significant in contemporary homiletics. Such preaching moves from law to gospel in a subtle and sophisticated manner. It is important to note that the word *law* may not explicitly appear in this preaching, but what law represents does appear. Law in such sermons is not merely a recitation of the commandments of God that we have lamentably failed to obey. It is an exposition of the emptiness and purposelessness to which contemporary humanity is prey. Law is an existential principle that represents both the dark side of human life and humanity's desire to justify itself before God by its own works.

Law, used in this manner, is more mirror than measuring stick. Gerhard Ebeling, a great Lutheran theologian and biblical scholar, wrote: "Law is for Luther not a revealed statutory norm . . . [but] an existentialist category which sums up the theological interpretation of man's being as it in fact is. Law is not therefore an idea or aggregate of principles, but *the reality of fallen man.*"[7] When we hold before our eyes the mirror of the law, we see our emptiness and fallenness. What is similar to the older preaching, however, is that failure comes first and motivates one to grasp the gospel. Our failure is demonstrated not so much by attempts to show that we have violated the law of God, but rather by pointing to signs of alienation, purposelessness, and a deep spiritual malaise in our society. This approach might be considered Luther as mediated by Paul Tillich. This appeal, inasmuch as it prepares the listener to hear and receive the gospel, carries out the same preparatory function as the older "strong needle of the law before the thread of the gospel." This kind of preaching has been practiced by many great North American preachers and is taught by some of our very best homileticians.[8]

Law/gospel preaching is biblical and is rooted in the preaching tradition of one of the mainstreams of the Christian church. It also works well and can be brilliantly persuasive in the mouths of some preachers. In particular, it can reach out "beyond the walls" to seekers and potential seekers. As such, it is rightly evangelistic. Those of us who live within the declining churches of historic Christianity had better begin to consider what is evangelistically effective. The matter is too important to be left to the strange voices that presently seem to pour forth like an ever rolling but muddy stream from our radios and televisions.

But reading Psalm 119 and many other passages of scripture with a sharp law/gospel distinction leaves one with a vague sense of discomfort. To the psalmist, the law is clearly a good and lovely gift from God. It is, indeed, a manifestation of the grace of God. It is a gift in itself and not merely a preparation for something else.

I do not think any Christian would want to say: "Happy are those whose way is blameless, who walk in the reality of fallen humankind" (see Ps. 119:1).

"Open my eyes, so that I may behold the reality of fallen humankind" (see Ps. 119:18). This at least makes sense, but, as a paraphrase, it violates the intent of the passage.

But, "the reality of fallen humankind is my delight" (see Ps. 119:77), or "O, how I love the reality of fallen humankind" make no sense whatsoever. Quite plainly, Psalm 119 operates with a different notion of the value and function of the law.

The reader will already have noted that in the parodies of selected verses of Psalm 119, I simply replaced the word *law* with the phrase *reality of fallen humankind* borrowed from Ebeling and slightly updated. It is, of course, immediately obvious that to do so is to violate the "feel" of the passages. Let me try again:

"Happy are those whose way is blameless, who walk in the gospel."

"Open my eyes that I may behold the gospel."

"The gospel is my delight." "O, how I love the gospel."

These make sense, and the "feel" is right. In fact, one could also substitute "gospel" for any of the key terms in Psalm 119. Let us revisit our section of the psalm for a minute:

Teach me your gospel.
I do not forget your gospel.
Your gospel is my heritage forever; it is the joy of my heart.

One can imagine pious Christians speaking just those words. Perhaps this is because law and its synonyms represent for the psalmist what gospel represents for the Christian—God's gracious way of dealing with humanity. If law, like gospel, is God's grace made present among us, then perhaps the length of the psalm is not merely tedium; it is the praise of one who knows that there is no limit to God's mercy. As a more recent psalmist has put it, "There's a wideness in God's mercy."

If we read Psalm 119 carefully, we are also reminded that the grace of God made present among us through the law functions as more than merely preparation for the hearing of the gospel. The most beloved and familiar words of our text assure us that the word of God, precisely as law, is a lamp to our feet and a light to our path. Here, law is neither hammer nor mirror, but rather a much-loved guide. This guide need not be dispensed with once we have come by the various paths of our lives to Christ. As the apostle Paul insists, we are not made righteous before God by obeying the law. The sinner is justified by the free grace of God made known in Jesus Christ, the substance of the gospel. In response to that grace, the justified sinner longs to live a life of grateful obedience both individually and socially. Such a life glorifies God and will benefit both the neighbor and ourselves. The law provides instruction in this freely undertaken task.[9] "The law thus lies in the gospel like the Tables of Sinai in the ark of the Covenant."[10] There are still perplexing paths to walk, and God's law will still enlighten us. As such, the Christian can say, with the psalmist, "The law is my delight" and "O, how I love the law."

PREACHING GRACE FROM PSALM 119

We now turn from a consideration of the relation of law and gospel in general to the challenges of preaching our text in particular. In the first place, the variety of vocabulary used in Psalm 119 suggests that we might also utilize in our preaching more than the simple term *law*. In so doing, we might help our listeners experience law as gracious gift. It may be helpful, for example, to use the Hebrew word *torah* when speaking of the law. We might point out that torah is not just regulation, but "instruction." Anyone who has struggled to assemble some complicated piece of machinery, install hardware on a computer, or even put together a child's toy on Christmas Eve, knows how helpful clear instruction from the "maker" actually can be. To be more accurate, it is when we do not have clear instructions that we recognize most clearly the value of the real thing. "Insert tab A into slot C" and so on. Therefore, "I do not forget your law."

By turning from a primarily negative use of the word *law*, we may inculcate in our people a greater respect for Judaism. Many of our people, though not overtly anti-Semitic, do tend to characterize Judaism as a religion in which salvation is earned as a reward for observing the manifold precepts of the law and therefore consider Jews legalistic. This is terribly unfair to Judaism. Judaism knows, as does Christianity, that we exist only within the divine mercy. It considers the Torah a gift of that mercy.

We might also emphasize not merely the "oughtness" of our duty to God, but also the power of God to enable us to do new and wonderful things. Because the word is a lamp to our feet and a light to our path, we are now able to walk confidently where previously we had stumbled about in the dark. In this respect, the law does not so much limit freedom as create it. In our preaching, we can emphasize possibility rather than precept. To be more specific, we may use "can" or "may" or "are able" rather than "must," "ought," or "are called to."

The many images of the word as lamp and light remind us that when preaching doctrine, it is of the first importance that we image such a sermon appropriately. The preacher does not merely identify images in the text. (That might be as interesting as a Friday afternoon high school English literature class.) The preacher also conveys new images to the listeners. Here is an effort on my part to image the notion that law as instruction gives new freedoms.

> I remember standing with my son Daniel at Cub Scouts. We were making a Christmas craft together on a parent-and-son evening. Our project was to construct a clothes rack, cut from one-inch thick wood, shaped to look like a reindeer's antlers. To cut the convoluted shape of the reindeer's antlers would be a difficult task for eight-year-old boys. For each parent-and-son pair, there was an electric jigsaw, a dangerous implement if handled carelessly. So we parents were to give *instruction* before beginning.
>
> I turned to Daniel and told him, "You could hurt yourself very badly with this. Don't let your fingers get anywhere near the blade. Keep your

hands above the wood at all times. Make sure the electric cord is out of the way of the blade." Many other things I said also to him. I spoke firmly, sternly. A passerby might even think I spoke fiercely. But Daniel knew me, and as he took electric saw in hand to do this new and wonderful thing and to do it safely, he looked at me with love in his eyes . . . and he quivered with delight.

The preacher will struggle with our society's ambivalence toward law as such. The preacher might begin, therefore, with a description of the spiritual and ethical uncertainties among which the pious Jew lived. This would take the form of a description of the standards and practices of the peoples around them. An example of this kind of description might be found in C. S. Lewis's *Reflections on the Psalms*.[11] Lewis's treatment perhaps poses too sharp a distinction between the Jews and their neighbors. The inhabitants of the eastern Mediterranean basin were not without ethical resources that could be called admirable under any standard. There was, however, a genuine distinction between the Jews and their neighbors, a distinction that was profoundly attractive to many non-Jews.

We might then move by way of analogy to our own situation. Surely there are ethical standards of great worth in our society that do not derive directly from the scriptures. (Many may, however, derive indirectly from them.) But what can we say about our society as a whole? Are not lack of purpose and normlessness hallmarks of our time? And is there not great misery?

By contrast, when the Jews turned to their law, they found something clean and clear and bracing, something worth living by. To them, it must have seemed a genuinely beautiful thing, "a lamp to the feet and a light to the path." Amidst the normlessness and purposelessness of our society, we too have not been left alone. We have been given torah, instruction. And more, we have been given an example of what it means to live by the weightier things of the law. And still more, we have been given the Holy Spirit to strengthen us and guide us and enable us to live by that law.

And so:

"Happy are those whose way is blameless, who walk in the law."
"Open my eyes that I may behold the law."
"The law is my delight."
"O, how I love the law."

CHAPTER 11

Isaiah 58:1-12: Grace and God's Justice

Noted theologian Miroslav Volf once wrote: "There is a profound 'injustice' about the God of the biblical traditions. It is called *grace.*"[1] This is one case in which the quotation marks are absolutely vital to the meaning of a sentence. Grace is only apparently an "injustice." If the God of grace demands justice, the two cannot be in contradiction. In our preaching, however, the two often sound very much like opposites. When we preach grace, we often seem to forget justice, and our preaching of justice is sometimes singularly graceless. Perhaps a study of Isaiah 58:1-12, a classic "justice" text, can help us preach justice with grace and grace with justice.

THE SETTING AND LIMITS OF THE TEXT

Many scholars call Isaiah 56 through 66 *Trito* or *Third Isaiah.* There are several ways to understand this part of the book of Isaiah. One way is to interpret these chapters in light of the likely circumstances of composition of the text, in short, to apply the traditional historical-critical method.[2] It is thought that this part of the book of Isaiah was composed shortly after the return of the exiles from Babylon to Jerusalem. When the exiles returned it was to a city in ruins. The temple lay in heaps of stones, not to be rebuilt for nearly a generation, and then only in an inferior fashion. The city walls would not be rebuilt for another century under the leadership of Nehemiah. Very probably the economy lay in ruins also. One might compare the situation to the former East Germany. When the

Berlin Wall came down, there was rejoicing in the streets, and the Berlin symphony orchestra played Beethoven's Ninth Symphony where the Wall once stood. But then economic reality set in—unemployment, high prices, and all. So it may have been for the returned exiles. They returned with joy to Zion, but once they arrived they had to live with the consequences of defeat and destruction. It could not have been easy for them.

In such a situation, it would be reasonable to imagine two consequences. The first consequence would be poverty, and the second would be complaints against God's management of human affairs. It is also argued by some scholars that the author of this part of Isaiah belonged to a circle that was in conflict with priests who strongly emphasized the liturgical and ritual life of the community. These folk supposed that a more correct and complete cultic life would please God and cause the Lord to rescue the people from their troubles. The prophet, however, seems to have had a different idea. Certainly, such a setting would help explain our text.

It is also possible to understand the book of Isaiah as a coherent whole rather than as a collection of disparate units springing from very different historical situations.[3] In its final form, Isaiah is but one book. Our text is part of a single work in which, it is said, a holy God has left only "a few survivors" (Isa. 1:9) of an unjust society that can only be "redeemed by justice" (Isa. 1:27). It is also a society to which God sends a prophet whose unclean lips are purified by a coal from the altar (Isa. 6:7), to whom God will say, "Comfort, comfort my people" (Isa. 40:1). To these very people God will say, "Seek the LORD, while he may be found" (Isa. 55:6). The book of Isaiah as a whole is a mixture of fierce rebuke and tender promise. So also is our passage. It is my intention to read the text both as a word to a very specific historical situation and as an integral part of the work as a whole.

The immediate context of our text is a mixture of demand and promise. So, for example, we hear in Isaiah 56:1, "Maintain justice, and do what is right, for soon my salvation will come." That mingled word continues through chapter 57. We hear, "Peace, peace, to the far and the near, says the LORD" (Isa. 57:19). Then, immediately before our text, comes a related but harder word, "There is no peace, says my God, for the wicked" (Isa. 57:21). The literary context prepares us to hear a mixed word. Perhaps the mixture contains both justice and grace.

It is not difficult to determine the beginning of our text. Isaiah 58:1 contains a command to the prophet to address the people on a new subject, the futility of their fasts. The prophetic word then continues as a coherent whole through at least verse 12. The conclusion of the unit is slightly more difficult to determine. Verses 13 and 14 might be considered a part of the same oracle, but, inasmuch as they chiefly concern a related but distinct matter, Sabbath-keeping, they could be considered separately from our text.

VERSES 1-3A, THE PEOPLE'S COMPLAINT—AND GOD'S

The passage begins with a command to preach: "Shout out, do not hold back! *Lift up your voice* like a trumpet!" The "trumpet" is actually the *shofar* or ram's horn, by no means a commonplace musical instrument, played chiefly for amusement. It was blown in war, as a signal or as summons to battle (see Josh. 6:5, Judg. 3:27, 1 Sam. 13:3 and many other examples). It was also used on solemn religious occasions such as the first day of the complex of feasts that leads to the Day of Atonement, Yom Kippur, for example. (Our text is the prescribed reading from the prophets for the Day of Atonement in at least some branches of Judaism.) The sound of the *shofar* announces that something momentous is to be said or done.

There may also be a deliberate echo here of similar words in Isaiah:

> Lift up your voice with strength,
> O Jerusalem, herald of good tidings,
> lift it up, do not fear;
> say to the cities of Judah,
> "Here is your God!" (Isa. 40:9)

We might certainly call that passage a command to preach grace. Here, by contrast, the message is, at first sight, anything but grace. Certainly, it is not a command to preach good news. The herald's voice had announced the return from exile in Isaiah 40. Very likely the return to a ruined city had not met the people's expectations. Far more important, however, the people had not met God's expectations. "With strength" is a mild translation of the command to preach. The preacher's job was to speak the word in a full-throated, "pound the pulpit" voice. The prophet's task is to tell the people that they were in a state of *rebellion*, a loaded word to those living under the authority of a powerful empire. The returned exiles need only look around them in the ruined city to see evidence of the consequences of rebellion. The nature of the rebellion is simple; it is sin. Nevertheless, it is important to note the description of those to whom this hard word will come. The hard word comes to "my people" and to the "house of Jacob." The first description is one of relationship. Rebels and sinners or not, they belong to God. The second description reminds the listeners of the history of salvation and God's promises to their ancestors. The word may be a word of judgment, but it is a word within the context of the covenant with Israel.

The prophet at first speaks of the people as if they were holy and righteous: "Yet day after day they seek me and delight to know my ways." Theirs is a false piety, however. The vital words here may be *as if*. Though they were in fact rebels, the people approached God *as if* they were a nation that practiced righteousness. The prophet, we might note, assumes that righteousness is primarily not a state, but an activity; it is practiced. Like justice, to which it is closely allied, righteousness can be *done*. But not only have the people not practiced righteousness, they have actively forsaken the ordinances of God.

The people would probably have agreed that righteousness is to be practiced. The problem was that they supposed they had done so. Indeed, their appeal is for *God* to practice righteousness: "They ask of me righteous judgments." The people delight in drawing near to God. This sounds *as if* it were obedience to God's invitation: "Seek the LORD while he may be found, call upon him while he is near" (Isa. 55:6). It is not; they draw near only to question and complain.

A student once said to me in class, "Some biblical criticism is like playing *Jeopardy*. It is trying to figure out the question to which the text is the answer." This usually poses a considerable challenge to the interpreter. In this case, however, the question is given to us. The people were asking, "Why do we fast, but you do not see? Why humble ourselves, but you do not notice?" In more contemporary language we might say, "We do all the right religious things. Why don't you answer our prayers?"

One of the "right religious things" is fasting. It was widely practiced in ancient Israel as a sign of sorrow and repentance. It was also intended to add a note of seriousness to prayer. So David fasted while praying for the life of his infant son by Bathsheba (2 Sam. 12:23). A whole community could hold a fast (1 Kings 21:9-12; Ezra 8:21-23; Esther 4:16). (The first example is particularly interesting since it is a fast used for an evil purpose.) The community, faced by many troubles after the return from the exile, hoped that their fast would draw God's attention.

Their complaint is similar in its language to the psalms of lament. Psalm 10:1 is a good example of this kind of language:

> Why, O LORD, do you stand far off?
> Why do you hide yourself in times of trouble?

In our preaching we often suggest, on the basis of these psalms of lament, that it is right and proper to make our complaints known to God. That is generally but not invariably true. Not all complaints are created equal. This complaint presupposes a relationship with God that is very similar to a business deal. For the people of Judah, fasting appears to be little more than a normally "profitable" religious investment on which they are not gaining a proper return.[4] They suppose that if they do the "right religious things" for God, God will be obligated to hear their prayers and bless them accordingly. The complaint of the people is wrongheaded for two reasons. In the first place, a right relationship with God is not nearly so businesslike. It actually depends not on the performance of a contract, but on grace. We shall return to this matter later. But second, as the text makes clear, the people are not, in truth, doing the "right religious things."

Verses 3b-5, the People's Fast

The people's fasts are not right religious things after all. In the first place, there are obvious violations—such as quarreling and fistfighting—of any kind of sober and decent religion. It's a "fast with a fist."[5] One might think in this connection of one of the more inglorious manifestations of "religion" in Northern Ireland, such as a Protestant march or an IRA funeral. Far too often prayers can degenerate into punches. It may be, by contrast, that there are few actual fistfights in North American churches, but we all know that quarreling is rife. There is, as a consequence, a small library of books and other resources on "conflict management" available these days.

It is not simply the obvious perversions of religion such as fistfights that are offensive to God, however. The more respectable manifestations of religion may also be objectionable. Even the standard displays of sorrow and repentance—sackcloth and ashes and prostration before God—can be displeasing to God. Right religious things merely offend God if they are not in truth the *right* religious things. The people have heard this from other prophets. See, for example, Micah 6:6-8 and Amos 5:21-24. None of these things create a "day acceptable to the Lord," another echo of Amos.

One further observation might be helpful: Through our text as a whole, references to God are in the third-person singular. That is to say, the prophet speaks of or for God. There are only two occurrences of God speaking in the first person, the first of which is in verse 5: "Is such the fast that I choose?" God's own voice breaks through even the prophet's words to declare what God abhors.

Verses 6-7, the Lord's Fast

The following verse begins with the only other instance in which God speaks in the first person: "Is not this the fast that I choose?" God's own voice breaks through a second time to declare now what God *demands*. In these verses, the prophet will tell us in a series of rhetorical questions just what actually constitutes the "right religious things" in God's sight. The words are clear, powerful, and immediately comprehensible. They do not so much require explanation as demand obedience.

There are, nevertheless, a few observations to be made here. In the first place, the Lord requires in these short verses both what we in our day would call justice and what we might call charity. (The Old Testament would probably call the latter "mercy.") The four acts mentioned in verse 6 all require struggle against injustice. Since this text is a piece of Hebrew poetry, a characteristic of which is parallelism, the four acts enjoined in verse 6 are likely interrelated. "To undo the thongs of the yoke, to let the oppressed go free, and to break every yoke" are different ways of saying, "loose the chains of injustice." Similarly, verse 7 as a whole is parallel to verse 6 as a whole. The structure—rhetorical question plus four acts of mercy—is almost identical. That is to say, the acts of charity, mentioned in verse 7, are essentially the same as the acts of justice in verse 6. The fact that the text moves so seamlessly from justice to charity may mean that our distinction between the two is an artificial one.

The distinction between justice and charity, though artificial and profoundly unbiblical, is sadly real in practice. It is quite possible to maintain and profit from the structures of injustice while engaging in personal or corporate acts of charity. It is easy, for example, to donate to a shelter for the homeless while upholding the system that makes homelessness inevitable. Similarly, it is entirely possible to be a tireless (and probably tiresome) advocate for "justice" without actively relieving the needs of the poor. Our text reminds us that this dichotomy will not do. The struggle against injustice and relief of human need are but one thing, the "fast" the Lord requires.

In a list, the first and last items are usually especially significant. We have already discussed the first words, "loose the bonds of injustice." The last words are equally interesting. A true fast is "not to hide yourself from your own kin." At the beginning of our text the hearers are called "the house of Jacob" and "my people." The prophet's word to them is based on a relationship, to be more exact, a covenant relationship. The relationship is not merely vertical, however; it is also horizontal. The poor, the naked, and the hungry are not nameless and faceless abstractions. Rather, they are "kin."

There are secular understandings of justice, which demand that it be as blind as the famous statue, scales in one hand, sword in the other, eyes blindfolded. In such understandings, a sense of connection and belonging would disrupt the disinterested calculations necessary to true justice.

Biblical justice is never disinterested but always inextricably *connected* to both God and the other. Justice is never a matter of calculation, but of compassion. The poor are not a nameless, faceless horde, but, in the profoundest sense, "kin."

Furthermore, the kind of indirect commands we find in this text are only necessary if the people are not actually performing these duties. In such a situation, they function not only as demands, but also as accusations. These words speak most directly in our time to analogous situations in which we fail to loose the bonds of injustice, break every yoke, share bread with the hungry, and so on. It will be all too easy for the preacher to identify those situations. Once again, the word will speak as demand and even as accusation. That is not the whole truth about these verses, however. I think of an inner-city mission in my own community. On its walls in a private area open only to the staff are lovely engravings of these very words from Isaiah. To be sure, they function there as a reminder to the staff of what the Lord requires of them. But, in truth, the people who work in that mission do everyday what the text requires. In that situation, the function of the text changes markedly; it becomes not accusation, but assurance. Those who live according to the demand of the word may claim the promise of the word. This leads us to the final section of our text.

VERSES 9-12, THE PROMISE

The prophet then speaks a word of promise. If you do all this, "your light shall break forth like the dawn" (Isa. 58:8). Light is a powerful image in Scripture as a whole and in the latter chapters of Isaiah in particular. God promises that Israel will be "a light to the nations" (Isa. 49:6). That light is closely connected to the justice of the Lord, "for a teaching will go out from me, and my justice for a light to the peoples" (Isa. 51:4). Where there is no justice, by contrast, there is no light, as in Isaiah 59:9: "Therefore justice is far from us, and righteousness does not reach us; we wait for light, and lo! there is darkness; and for brightness, but we walk in gloom." When justice and mercy are done, however, then light itself inevitably breaks forth.

The word *light* ends the first half of the line in Hebrew. The second half of the line begins with the word *healing*. This arrangement, called a chiasm, throws into prominence these two key words. The image of healing, expressed in many different ways, is almost as significant in Scripture as light. The particular Hebrew word behind *healing* is not common in Isaiah nor indeed in the Old Testament as a whole, though it serves as an image of restoration after exile in the "Book of Consolation" of Jeremiah (33:6).

Healing as an image is, however, a powerful one in Scripture. The particular word refers to the slow healing over of a wound. It is a "gradual process, not an instantaneous transformation of the whole scene."[6]

The words *your light* and *your healing* could be misunderstood. It cannot be emphasized too strongly that neither the light nor the healing belongs to the people. The light is "their" light in that it will illumine them. The healing is likewise "theirs" in that, by the mercy of God, they will experience healing. Both light and healing come, in the beginning, from God.

The promise then echoes the journey language, which is a constant feature of Isaiah 40 through 55, words of promise written to exiles in Babylon. Though most scholars suppose that the exiles have already returned to Jerusalem by the time our text was written, the language is still powerful. The ultimate source of all this imagery, wherever it is found in Isaiah, is the story of the exodus. The people of God in all times and places must always consider themselves as if they themselves were those whom the Lord had brought out of Egypt and through the wilderness (cf. Deut. 5:3). Even in a settled city, it is still possible to travel, and God will accompany that pilgrimage also.

The "vindicator" (NRSV) will go before them and the "glory of the Lord" will be their rear guard. The translation is both simple and difficult at this point. The "glory of the Lord" is a common phrase in the Bible, perhaps most familiar to us from the Christmas story in the Gospel of Luke. The glory, here as in that familiar passage, is God's awesome and gracious presence. The Hebrew word behind *vindicator* is also simple. It is the Hebrew word usually translated *righteousness,* as, for example, in verse 2 of our text or in the RSV of this verse. It is, however, a word with a rich and complex range of meanings. Sometimes the word *righteousness* is almost a synonym for *salvation,* and so it is here. It is God's gracious will to be in such close relationship with the people that they will be surrounded by the saving presence of God. From the structure of the verse, it appears that these two concepts—glory and righteousness—are parallel. In other words, the "righteousness" that will go before the people is not a righteousness that is their own achievement. The righteousness is no more the people's accomplishment than is the glory.

In this kind of relationship, the people will call and God will answer. There is a play on words in the Hebrew that cannot be reproduced in English.[7] The verb *to answer* is identical in spelling to the verb *to be bowed down or afflicted.* That verb or its derivatives lie behind no less than four English words in our text—the self-humbling of verses 3 and 5, and the poor or afflicted of verses 7 and 10. An inadequate attempt to get at the significance of the play on words might be:

Though you may think you're humble,
Your prayer's just a mumble
Unless you turn to the humble.

The answer that God will give is truly lovely: "Here I am." It is a word that God longs to say: "I was ready to be sought out by those who did not ask, to be found by those who did not seek me. I said, 'Here I am, here I am,' to a nation that did not call on my name" (Isa. 65:1). When justice is done, nothing can stand in the way of that word. Indeed, in the glorious future that God promises, the day will come when it is not necessary even to call upon the Lord: "Before they call I will answer, while they are yet speaking I will hear" (Isa. 65:24). In the end, the promise is not simply material blessing. It is the assurance of an abiding presence. We are never alone on the journey. This is beginning to sound like grace after all.

The prophet then circles back in verses 9*b* and 10*a* to the conditions for blessing. The conditions divide naturally into two parts, abstaining from evil and performing the good. All this will happen, says the prophet, "if you remove the yoke from among you, the pointing of the finger, the speaking of evil, if you offer your food to the hungry and satisfy the needs of the afflicted." The first half of the condition adds something new. Community can be shattered by cruel words and hurtful gestures as much as by indifference or even active cruelty. We learn a ludicrous untruth in childhood: "Sticks and stones may break my bones, but words will never hurt me." The prophet knows better. Justice is as much a matter of the tongue and the finger as of the hand.

The second part of the condition, as we read it in the NRSV, seems to restate in slightly different language the material in verse 7. The Hebrew does not, however, say "if you offer your *food* to the hungry," but rather your *nephesh*, your self. The RSV ("If you pour yourself out for the hungry . . . ") or the NIV ("If you spend yourselves in behalf of the hungry . . . ") catch the meaning more vigorously. The wrong sort of charity can have a distancing effect, separating us from those we suppose we are assisting. Disconnected charity is no charity at all. In truth, there is no substitute for the self in giving.

If all this is done, the blessing of the Lord will flow. The prophet here speaks some of the loveliest imagery in all Scripture. Once again, "your light shall rise in the darkness and your gloom be like the noonday" (cf. v. 8). God will "guide you continually and satisfy your need in parched places." This also is exodus language. Even the bones, the inner self, will then be made strong. In that day, moreover, "you shall be like a watered garden, like a spring of water, whose waters never fail." Water is in all places and, most obviously in arid countries, a necessity of life. It also symbolized the presence of God in Scripture. In that day, there will be true urban renewal: "Your ancient ruins shall be rebuilt; you shall raise up the foundations of many generations; you shall be called the repairer of the breach, the restorer of streets to live in." This must have been a truly lovely picture to the returned exiles squatting amidst the ruined splendor of Jerusalem.

PREACHING GRACE FROM ISAIAH 58

Preaching grace does not mean evading or softening the challenge of a text. The hard word of this text must be spoken and spoken clearly. In the first place, we must not suppose that we in the church are immune from the stinging critique of Isaiah 58 simply because, by and large, we do not fast, wear sackcloth, or pour ashes on our heads. We too are careful to practice what we suppose are the right religious things. (Indeed, as a professor of preaching and worship, I am hired by my denomination to ensure that new ministers can perform the right religious things with suitable efficiency and grace.) Our religious practices might likewise be offensive in God's eyes. God demands justice not only of the returned exiles, but also of us. A faithful preacher may not shirk the task of preaching a hard word.

There is, however, promise as well as demand in our text. Having spoken the hard word, we may also point to the promise. The difficulty with doing so, however, is that the text appears to make God's blessing conditional upon our performance. The relationship with God might indeed seem to be akin to a business deal. The only difference between the people and the prophet, under such an understanding, would be that the prophet understands the terms of the deal properly. The inhabitants of Judah suppose that it is acts of contrition that please God though the prophet knows that God honors only acts of justice and mercy. Taken in one way, the text sounds not unlike the words of Job's friends: "Your problems come from doing the wrong things. If you do the right ones you will be healed." If that were so, we could preach justice from this text, but not grace.

The text might be read and preached in that way but it need not. There are, in fact, clues in the text itself that another reading is possible. It is clear from the text that God is favorably disposed toward the poor. The Lord demands on their behalf both justice and mercy. God is not, however, favorably disposed only to the poor. We return to the beginning of the text. It is a word to "my people" and to "the house of Jacob." Even in the midst of full-throated condemnation, Judah remains the covenant people of God. The people of Judah, rebellious sinners though they may be, are in relationship with God. God longs for the relationship to be strengthened and deepened, to be able to bless them in every way and to say to them, "Here I am." All this is spoken, moreover, while the people are in a state of rebellion or, as the apostle Paul might say, while they were yet sinners. The relationship within which both condemnation and promise are spoken rests not upon human performance, but upon God's favorable disposition toward the people. That favorable disposition is, of course, grace.

All this might also be a clue to the relationship between justice and grace. Grace is certainly not the opposite of justice. It is, in fact, injustice that blocks the flow of grace. Justice, by contrast, allows grace to reach out to all the people, even to those who by their acts of injustice have previously blocked its flow. When this happens, the relationship among people is restored. The rich and the poor are once again "kin." And in that restoration, the relationship with God is also renewed. Once again, those who heed God's command will hear the gracious words of assurance, "Here I am." Our task when preaching this text is to demand justice, but to do so within a relationship of grace. What is explicitly true about our text, moreover, that the demand for justice is spoken within a relationship based on grace, is implicitly true of all other justice texts as well. This suggests that all our preaching of justice can be colored by grace.

Our text also shows us that justice is as lovely and as desirable as the images of blessing that fill the second half of our text. It is water in a parched land, light amidst the gloom, and children playing in the streets of a restored city. Justice need not be preached merely as a grim, teeth-gritting duty. The preacher can rehearse these captivating images and create new ones that are appropriate to our time. Our text lays on us the duty of preaching justice but doing so graciously. (That too applies to more than this text.)

We have, in a way, come full circle in this book and returned to our first text, 2 Corinthians 8. There, Paul reminds the Corinthian Christians, his brothers and sisters or his kin, of the grace of the Lord Jesus. He does so in order to move them to care for the needs of the poor of Jerusalem. I like to think that the prophet who told his listeners to share bread with the hungry of Jerusalem and to bring the homeless poor into their house would have approved. Grace and a care for others, a care manifest in both justice and mercy, can never be separated.

Coda

I have used the story of Professor Kelly and the twenty-dollar bill many times over the years, with many different groups. I always give away a bill, though sometimes not a twenty, and only occasionally has the recipient tried to give the money back to me later. I always figure that anybody who tries to do that has missed the point. But usually they get it.

On one occasion, I was teaching a class of candidates for the office of permanent deacon in the Roman Catholic Archdiocese of Toronto. Normally in the Roman Catholic Church, the diaconate is a way station on the road to the priesthood. But recently the authorities, perhaps motivated by the shortage of priestly vocations, have recruited married men to be educated as deacons and to remain in that office for life. These permanent deacons are then able to relieve the priests of a considerable number of their duties. Because this is a new program and the candidates are very carefully screened, the group is always made up of high quality people. I thoroughly enjoy teaching them. As I expected, the chosen "victim" received the bill, this time a ten, with "good grace."

The day after the program ended, I went down to my office. The program takes place out of the academic term, and my trip was unplanned. To my surprise, I saw one of the permanent deacon candidates, in fact, the one to whom I had given the money, bending down and slipping an envelope under my office door. He looked very embarrassed when he saw me. I greeted him politely, of course. He flushed, handed me the envelope, mumbled something about wanting to thank me for my part in the program and bolted out the door. I assumed there was a thank-you card in the envelope, thought, "How kind!" and began the administrivial duties that had taken me down to my office.

When I had finished my tasks, I finally got around to opening the envelope. There was no card but inside was a folded piece of notepaper. On the outside was written, "Mark 4:20. And some seed fell on good soil; they hear the word and accept and bear fruit, thirty and sixty and hundredfold."

Inside the notepaper was a thousand-dollar bill.

Call it grace and grace still surprises.

Notes

Introduction

1. Nowadays, a student might advance a suitably contemporary political interpretation that children are marginalized and have no power. I doubt if Professor Kelly would have been impressed. Children were valued in the world of the scriptures of Israel. "Blessed are those whose quiver is full of them!" Though a child might have no power, if he (the gender specific pronoun is intended) was the son of a wealthy family, he would inherit wealth and power in due course. That is the point of Paul's comparison of the law to the *paidogogos*, the slave who temporarily bore authority over the heir. If Mark's Jesus had intended to say that his followers must identify with the marginalized and oppressed, there would have been far easier and clearer ways to say so.

2. Anders Nygren, *Agape and Eros,* trans. Philip S. Watson (London: SPCK, 1953), 83-84.

3. I believe that the most important influence on the preaching of students is not their professor, but the preachers of their childhood and youth. After all, they have listened to these people many more hours than they have listened to their professors of homiletics.

4. David Buttrick, *A Captive Voice: The Liberation of Preaching* (Louisville, Ky.: Westminster/John Knox Press, 1994), 110.

5. I have told this story previously in my book *Preaching That Matters: The Bible and Our Lives* (Louisville, Ky.: Westminster/John Knox Press, 1998), 93-94.

6. It is hard to imagine a better collection of anecdotes and stories about grace than Philip Yancey's *What's So Amazing About Grace?* (Grand Rapids: Zondervan Publishing House, 1997).

7. Mary Catharine Hilkert, *Naming Grace: Preaching and the Sacramental Imagination* (New York: Continuum, 1998).

8. On this matter, see Paul S. Wilson, *God Sense: Reading the Bible for Preaching* (Nashville: Abingdon Press, 2001).

9. I deal with some of these questions in an essay, "Limping Away with a Blessing: Biblical Studies and Preaching at the End of the Second Millennium," *Interpretation* 51 (1997): 358-70.

10. Dietrich Bonhoeffer, *The Cost of Discipleship*, trans. R. H. Fuller (New York: Macmillan, 1959), 36.

11. Michael Kesterton, *The Toronto Globe and Mail*, 13 April 2000, A 24.

1. 2 CORINTHIANS 8:7-15: YOU KNOW THE GRACE OF OUR LORD JESUS

1. Ernest Best (in *Second Corinthians* [Atlanta: John Knox Press, 1987], 2) argues that 2 Corinthians 10–13 comes from a letter written after our 2 Corinthians 1–9, in other words, a Fifth Corinthians (at least)!

2. A thorough presentation of the various scholarly theories can be found in Hans Dieter Betz, *2 Corinthians 8 and 9: A Commentary on Two Administrative Letters of the Apostle Paul*, ed. George W. MacRae (Philadelphia: Fortress Press, 1985), 3-36.

3. Ibid.

4. So writes the seventeenth-century Puritan commentator Matthew Henry, as quoted in Betz, *2 Corinthians 8 and 9*, 9. Matthew Henry divided the text in the same manner as our lectionary reading.

5. See the treatment of this point on pages 32-34.

6. James Thompson, *Preaching Like Paul: Homiletical Wisdom for Today* (Louisville, Ky.: Westminster/John Knox Press, 2001), 54-55. At this point, Thompson is speaking primarily of Paul's custom of reminding the churches of what they already know about Paul himself and his ministry with them. This strategy is even more obvious with respect to the work of Christ (p. 145).

7. See my sermon with this title, on Second Corinthians 8:1-9, in my book *Preaching That Matters: The Bible and Our Lives* (Louisville, Ky.: Westminster/John Knox Press, 1998).

2. A WORD TO PHILEMON: GRACE TO YOU AND PEACE

1. This "story" was originated by Peter Lampe in "Keine 'Sklavenflucht des Onesimus,'" *Zeitschrift fur die Neutestamentliche Wissenschaft* 76 (1985): 135-37. Lampe's theory has been influential and has been summarized in various English-language sources. One thorough and easily accessible presentation can be found in B. M. Rapske, "The Prisoner Paul in the Eyes of Onesimus," *NTS* 37 (1991): 187-203. This theory has been adopted in the most recent major commentary on Philemon, James D. G. Dunn, *The Epistles to the Colossians and Philemon* (Grand Rapids: Eerdmans, 1996), 304-7. The basis of the theory in Roman law has been severely questioned by several classics scholars, however. See, for example, the study of J. Albert Harrill, "Using the Roman Jurists to Interpret Philemon: A Response to Peter Lampe," *ZNW* 90 (1999): 135-38.

2. John Knox, *Philemon Among the Letters of Paul: A New View of Its Place and Importance* (Chicago: University of Chicago Press, 1935).

3. Allen Dwight Callahan, "Paul's Epistle to Philemon: Toward an Alternative *Argumentum*," *Harvard Theological Review* 86 (1993): 357-76.

4. F. Forrester Church, "Rhetorical Structure and Design in Paul's Letter to

Philemon," *HTR* 19 (1978): 22. See page 17 note 3 for references to the various attempts to set the letter within the conventions of classical rhetoric.

5. The only other epistle in which Paul does not call himself apostle is Philippians, also a letter written from prison.

6. André Resner Jr., *Preacher and Cross: Person and Message in Theology and Rhetoric* (Grand Rapids: Eerdmans, 1999).

7. John M. Barclay, "Paul, Philemon and Christian Slave Ownership," *New Testament Studies* 37 (1961): 180-81.

8. Andrew Wilson, "The Pragmatics of Politeness and Pauline Epistolography: A Case Study of the Letter to Philemon," *JSNT* 48 (1992): 107-19.

9. Barclay, "Paul, Philemon and Christian Slave Ownership," 175.

10. Ibid., 186.

11. A similar thought appears in James Tunstead Burtchaell, *Philemon's Problem: A Theology of Grace* (Grand Rapids: Eerdmans, 1998), 30.

12. Ignatius, Epistle to the Ephesians, 1:6-8.

13. Douglas H. Rollwage in a sermon preached at the head offices of the Presbyterian Church in Canada.

3. EPHESIANS 2:1-10: BY GRACE YOU ARE SAVED, THROUGH FAITH

1. Howard Clark Kee, *The New Testament in Context: Sources and Documents* (Englewood Cliffs, N.J.: Prentice-Hall, 1984), 44.

2. I wrote the first draft of this chapter well before September 11, 2001 and revised it shortly after. It may be that after the terrible events of that day, Westerners are more ready to accept the notion of radical evil in which we are all involved. It may even be that some listeners are more ready to accept symbolism that connects evil with the heights above us.

3. *Kindness*, like *grace*, is a favorite word of Paul. Indeed, the Greek word here rendered *kindness* is only found in Scripture in Paul and in the Deutero-Pauline writings.

4. Our verse 5 and verse 8 clearly refer to the act of being saved as a past event. For "being saved" as an ongoing process, see 1 Corinthians 1:18: "For the message about the cross is foolishness to those who are perishing, but to us who are being saved it is the power of God." For an example of the future use of the verb, see Romans 5:10: "For if while we were enemies, we were reconciled to God through the death of his Son, much more surely, having been reconciled, will we be saved by his life."

5. Note that the author does not explicitly link works to the law as Paul does in Romans and Galatians. Those discussions are doubtless in the author's mind, however.

6. John Calvin, *The Epistles of Paul to the Galatians, Ephesians, Philippians, and Colossians*, trans. T. H. L. Parker (Edinburgh: Oliver and Boyd, 1965), 144. The exact quotation is "Faith, then, brings a man etc."

4. JOHN 5:1-18: BUT DO YOU WANT TO GET WELL?

1. Note that Raymond Brown in his classic commentary on the Gospel of John assigns verses 17 and 18 to the discourse (Raymond Brown, *The Gospel According to John, I-XII, The Anchor Bible*, vol. 29 [Garden City, N.Y.: Doubleday, 1966], 212-21).

2. The feasts appear to be a linking device in this part of the Gospel of John. So much is this the case that Raymond Brown in his classic commentary entitled this section of the Gospel "Jesus and the Principal Feasts of the Jews" (*John*, 200).

3. I can bear personal witness to the staying power of this childhood reading. In preparing this chapter, I read the passage through several times in both Greek and English before I even noticed the explanation wasn't there! I simply read it as if it were. I believe we all engage in these "as if" readings. That is why careful exegesis is always necessary.

4. John Sanford, *Mystical Christianity: A Psychological Commentary on the Gospel of John* (New York: Crossroad, 1993), 133.

5. Alexandra Gill, "Note to Self: Change Life Now," *The Toronto Globe and Mail*, 1 January 2000. (Note the date!)

6. Ibid.

7. Ibid.

8. Michael Card, *The Parable of Joy: Reflections on the Wisdom of the Book of John* (Nashville: Thomas Nelson Publishers, 1995), 66.

9. Sanford, *Mystical Christianity*, 136.

5. MARK 7:24-30: CRUMBS UNDER THE TABLE

1. With respect to literary patterns in the Gospel of Mark, an invaluable resource for the preacher is Robert Reid, *Preaching Mark* (St. Louis: Chalice, 1999).

2. With respect to some of these questions, see my essay "Limping Away with a Blessing: Biblical Studies and Preaching at the End of the Second Millennium," *Interpretation* 51 (1997): 358-70.

3. See my book *Preaching That Matters: The Bible and Our Lives* (Louisville, Ky.: Westminster/John Knox Press, 1998).

4. See ibid., 125-28 for a brief discussion of this mode of preaching.

5. This is the translation of the prayer that appears in *The Authorized Daily Prayer Book of the United Hebrew Congregations of the British Empire* (London: Eyre & Spottiswoode, 1925), 5-6.

6. See, for example, Bonnie Bowman Thurston, *Preaching Mark* (Minneapolis: Augsburg Fortress Press, 2002), 88.

7. I do not claim any great success for the sermon behind this chapter. Sometime later, Linda told me that the elders had got together and agreed, "Next year, let's get somebody from around here to preach anniversary Sunday." Oh well.

6. LUKE 19:1-10: TO SEEK AND TO SAVE THE LOST

1. Luke Timothy Johnson is correct in noting the similarities between the prophet Jesus and the prophet Moses in Luke's presentation, and also in denying "a careful imitation of the narrative of Deuteronomy." According to Johnson, the travel narrative has "a structure that is relatively simple but which serves Luke's narrative purposes well" (*The Gospel of Luke* [Collegeville, Minn.: Liturgical Press, 1991], 163).

2. See in this connection, Luke Timothy Johnson, *The Literary Function of Possessions in Luke-Acts* (Missoula, Mont.: Scholars Press, 1977).

3. In fact, Luke's Jesus appears to be a good deal more interested in money than sex, something one might not be able to guess from the present preoccupations of our churches. This is not to suggest that either Jesus or Luke would approve of our society's increasingly antinomian attitude to matters sexual. The absence of comment on such matters may well have resulted because the church inherited

without alteration or debate the Old Testament's standards with respect to sexuality. All this does suggest, however, that our focus may be misplaced if we so concentrate on the sexual that we forget the financial.

4. Charles H. Talbert rightly recognizes 18:31–19:44 as a unit (*Reading Luke: A Literary and Theological Commentary on the Third Gospel* [New York: Crossorad, 1984]. 175). But the claimed structural parallels to 17:11–18:30 are overstated. Moreover, the arrival in Jerusalem in 19:28-44 shows that this pericope is also part of the passion narrative. The section as a whole and the triumphal entry in particular have a hinge function in the structure of the Gospel.

5. Hans Conzelmann in his groundbreaking work of redaction criticism (*The Theology of St. Luke,* trans. G. Buswell [New York: Harper & Bros., 1961]) notes the peculiarity of the route and argues that it results from Luke's ignorance of Palestinian geography. This may well not be a correct deduction. It may simply be that Luke is more interested in theology than geography.

6. This is a fine phrase coined by Raymond Bailey in Roger Van Harn ed., *The Lectionary Commentary: Theological Exegesis for Sunday's Texts,* vol. III, *The Gospels* (Grand Rapids: Eerdmans, 2001), 437.

7. LUKE 19:11-27: GRACE MULTIPLYING

1. For those not familiar with the work of the Jesus Seminar, the "fifth" gospel is the Gospel of Thomas. The Jesus Seminar rates the parable considered in this paper as a "pink" passage, that is, as a passage that "sure sounds like Jesus" (Robert W. Funk, Roy W. Hoover, and the Jesus Seminar, *The Five Gospels: What Did Jesus Really Say?* [San Francisco: HarperCollins, 1993], 37, 373-75). The Seminar, in line with some older historical-critical scholarship, believes, however that Luke has combined two different stories. (So see, among others, Joachim Jeremias, *The Parables of Jesus,* 2nd ed. [New York: Charles Scribner's Sons, 1972], 59). Joseph Fitzmyer traces this theory back to Adolf von Harnack and Julius Wellhausen but gives no specific bibliographical references (*The Anchor Bible: The Gospel According to Luke X-XXIV* [Garden City, N.Y.: Doubleday, 1985], 1231). These are a "throne claimant" story and a parable, paralleled in Matthew, in which servants are entrusted with coins. A conservative scholar, Craig Blomberg, on the other hand, engages in a detailed study of the text in order to show that Jesus might have told the story in more or less its Lukan form on an occasion different from that recounted in Matthew (*Interpreting the Parables* [Downers Grove, Ill.: InterVarsity Press, 1990], 214-21). It is not my intention to debate these proposals.

2. Among the scholars who interpret Luke's parables in this manner are, Charles H. Talbert, *Reading Luke: A Literary and Theological Commentary on the Third Gospel* (New York: Crossroad, 1984); Robert C. Tannehill, *The Narrative Unity of Luke-Acts: A Literary Interpretation* (Philadelphia: Fortress Press, 1986); and Luke Timothy Johnson, who in his recent commentary on the Third Gospel also interprets the Lukan parables in a like manner. As a general policy and in connection with this parable in particular, Johnson states that he has taken "a literary approach to Luke's narrative, seeking to understand the form and function of specific passages within the literary and religious concerns of the narrative" (*The Gospel of Luke* [Collegeville, Minn.: Liturgical Press, 1991], 292).

3. It would be interesting to arrange to have the unit as a whole read aloud just as the passion story is read as a whole during Holy Week in some liturgical traditions. A sustained reading of larger segments of the Gospel than the short pericopes we normally hear can be immensely powerful.

4. The literary context in Matthew is also substantially different. There the parable of the talents leads into the apocalyptic discourse. The setting in Matthew is likewise a clue to meaning. There the parable ought to be interpreted eschatologically.

5. Jeremias, *The Parables of Jesus,* 59

6. The literary setting also casts doubt on the interpretation of this parable in N. T. Wright, *Jesus and the Victory of God* (Minneapolis: Fortress Press, 1996), 634-35. Wright argues that the parable is about the return of YHWH to Zion as king. Wright may be correct that YHWH will return to Zion, but the sign of that return is the coming of the King who comes in the name of the Lord, the son of David, Jesus himself.

7. See Brad H. Young, *The Parables: Jewish Tradition and Christian Interpretation* (Peabody, Mass.: Hendrickson, 1998), 82.

8. On the conflation of the two parables see note 1 of this chapter above.

9. "Gains of one thousand percent are thus more likely hyperbole than commonplace and calculated to draw an astonished gasp from the listening audience" (Richard L. Rohrbaugh, "A Peasant Reading of the Parable of the Talents/Pounds: A Text of Terror?" *Biblical Theology Bulletin* 23 (1993): 35. The hyperbole is theological. An interesting general background to the social setting of this parable can be found in Jerome H. Neyrey, ed., *The Social World of Luke-Acts* (Peabody, Mass.: Hendrickson, 1991). See especially Douglas E. Oakman, "The Countryside in Luke-Acts," 151-80.

10. Dominick Crossan claimed that there was a "normalcy" about this parable in his important work, *In Parables: The Challenge of the Historical Jesus* (San Francisco: Harper & Row, 1973), 102. I believe this is a serious misreading of the text.

11. Rohrbaugh, "A Peasant Reading of the Parable of the Talents/Pounds: *A Text of Terror?"* (italics mine).

12. For that matter, the parable is not an exact allegory of the career of Archelaus. For one thing, Archelaus slaughtered the political opposition, not the less ambitious among his servants.

13. On this point, see Rohrbaugh, "A Peasant Reading of the Parable of the Talents/Pounds: A Text of Terror?" 32-39.

8. Genesis 4:1-16: The Blood That Cries Out

1. Ann Weems, *Putting the Amazing Back in Grace* (Louisville: Westminster/John Knox Press, 1999), 10.

2. Philip Yancey, *What's So Amazing About Grace?* (Grand Rapids, Mich.: Zondervan Publishing House, 1997), 41.

3. *Authorized Daily Prayer Book of the United Hebrew Congregations of the British Empire,* 13th ed., 7.

4. Emil Schürer, *The History of the Jewish People in the Age of Jesus Christ,* rev. and ed. Geza Vermes, Fergus Millar, and Matthew Black (Edinburgh: T. & T. Clark, 1979), 2:456-57. This is drawn from the Babylonian version of that prayer.

5. *TDNT* IX, 381-87.

6. Reinhold Niebuhr, *The Nature and Destiny of Man,* vol. 1, *Human Nature* (New York: Charles Scribner's Sons, 1941), 269.

7. I completed the final draft of this chapter as the United States government was initiating the bombing of Afghanistan in response to the terrorist attacks of September 11, 2001. The awareness of a history that leads to violence is very strong at present.

8. Walter Brueggeman, *Genesis,* 261-62

9. New York: Warner Books, 1987.

10. The sermon was preached in a Christian Reformed Church in which the heritage of John Calvin is honored. It might be noted in this connection that there is also a troubling arbitrariness to the traditional Reformed doctrine of election. "I will have mercy on whom I have mercy" (Rom. 9:15). "Jacob have I loved but Esau have I hated" (Mal. 1:2, 3 KJV). Yet another pair of brothers is divided by the divine favor.

11. Paul A. Riemann, "Am I My Brother's Keeper?" *Interpretation* 24 (1970): 488.

12. Gunther Plaut, "Cain and Abel: Bible, Tradition, and Contemporary Reflection" in *Preaching Biblical Texts: Expositions by Jewish and Christian Scholars,* ed. Frederick C. Holmgren and Herman E. Schaalman (Grand Rapids, Mich.: Eerdmans, 1995), 15.

13. Ibid. The relevant passage can be found in Jacob Neusner, *Genesis Rabbah: The Judaic Commentary to the Book of Genesis: A New American Translation,* vol. 1 (Atlanta: Scholars Press, 1985), 250.

14. Sidney Greidanus, *Preaching Christ from the Old Testament* (Grand Rapids, Mich.: Eerdmans, 1999).

15. This is one insight of many that I owe to my former colleague at Knox College, Dr. Stanley Walters.

9. 2 Kings 5:1-14 (15-27): And None Was Healed Except Naaman

1. I am heavily influenced in my reading of this passage, particularly in believing that it contains deliberately comic elements, by the fine commentary in the *Interpretation* series of Richard Nelson, *First and Second Kings* (Louisville: John Knox Press, 1987).

2. A purely narrative reading of the text is sometimes not adequate. Traditional historical-critical question such as, "For whom was this text written?" often remain useful and important, not simply as academic exercises, but for preaching also.

3. Nelson, *First and Second Kings,* 176-77.

4. There is some evidence that it was supposed that kings could be channels of divine blessing. John Gray, *I & II Kings* (Philadelphia: Westminster Press, 1970), 505, note b. As late as the seventeenth century, it was widely believed in England that a condition called the "King's evil" could be cured by the monarch's touch.

5. Listeners distressed by the punishment might note that the servant is apparently healthy in 2 Kings 6 and 8. The punishment is largely a literary rounding off of the story. Once that is achieved, the narrator does not hold Gehazi in his misery.

10. Psalm 119: The Law As Gospel

1. A woman in Canada who felt that she must have an entirely pain-free experience of childbirth, no matter what risk to herself or to her infant, sued her doctors and the hospital when this was not provided. According to news reports, she had expected to be able to knit or read a magazine during the birthing process.

2. C. S. Lewis, *Reflections on the Psalms* (London: Fontana Books, 1961), 49.

3. Artur Weiser, *The Psalms* (Philadelphia: Westminster Press, 1962), 739.

4. Ibid.

5. James Luther Mays, *Psalms, Interpretation: A Bible Commentary for Teaching and Preaching* (Louisville: John Knox Press, 1994), 382.

6. Perhaps the most helpful resource on this subject is a work by Herman G. Stuempfle, *Preaching Law and Gospel* (Philadelphia: Fortress Press, 1978), 23-25. Stuempfle derives the image of the hammer from Martin Luther's phrase, a "large and powerful hammer." He derives the image of the mirror from Paul Tillich. The image is considerably older than Tillich, however. John Calvin, in his treatment of the uses of the law, writes: "The law is like a mirror. In it we contemplate our weakness, the iniquity rising from this and finally the curse coming from both— just as a mirror shows us the spots on our face" (*Institutes of the Christian Religion* II, vii).

7. Gerhard Ebeling, "On the Doctrine of the *Triplex Usus Legi* in the Theology of the Reformation," in *Word and Faith,* trans. James W. Leitch (Philadelphia: Fortress Press, 1963), 75.

8. Paul Scott Wilson in his earlier writings used "law and gospel" language. In a later work, *The Practice of Preaching* ([Nashville: Abingdon Press, 1995], 110ff.), he substitutes for "law" and "gospel," the categories "judgment" and "grace." Such changes in terminology may combat our overly negative understanding of law. Eugene Lowry also teaches a two-movement sermon pattern (*The Homiletical Plot: The Sermon as Narrative Art Form* [Atlanta: John Knox Press, 1980]).

9. Some readers will recognize that this is a characteristically Reformed way of understanding the law. John Calvin called it the "third and principal use which pertains more closely to the proper purpose of the law" (Calvin, *Institutes of the Christian Religion* II, vii, 12). (The first two uses are as "mirror" and as a restraint upon the evildoer. It is significant that immediately after enunciating the "third and principal use," Calvin quotes Psalm 19 and then likewise, "Thy word is a lamp to my feet and a light to my path" (Ps. 119:105) *and innumerable other sayings in the same psalm*" (italics mine) (Calvin, *Institutes of the Christian Religion* II, vii, 12). It is not, however, an understanding that is unique to the Reformed tradition. Indeed, it may have first appeared in Protestant theology in the work of Luther's successor Philip Melanchthon.

10. The quotation is from the essay "Gospel and Law" in *Community, State, and Church; Three Essays* by Karl Barth (Garden City, N.Y.: Doubleday), 80.

11. Lewis, *Reflections on the Psalms,* 55.

11. Isaiah 58:1-12: Grace and God's Justice

1. Miroslav Volf, *Exclusion and Embrace: A Theological Exploration of Identity, Otherness, and Reconciliation* (Nashville: Abingdon Press, 1996), 221.

2. See Elizabeth Achtemeier, *The Community and Message of Isaiah 56–66: A Theological Commentary* (Minneapolis: Augsburg, 1982), 11-28.

3. For a fine example of this kind of reading, see Edgar W. Conrad, *Reading Isaiah* (Minneapolis: Fortress Press, 1991).

4. Philippe Kabongo-Mbaya quoted in Stephen Farris and Paraic Reamonn, eds., *Break the Chains of Injustice: Bible Studies for the 23rd General Council* (Geneva: World Alliance of Reformed Churches, 1997), 18.

5. Johanna Van Wijk-Bos quoted in Farris and Reamonn, *Break the Chains of Injustice,* 24.

6. Claus Westermann, *Isaiah 40–66,* trans. David M. G. Stalker (Philadelphia: Westminster Press, 1969), 338.

7. Van Wijk-Bos, *Break the Chains of Injustice,* 48.